Not Afraid of Flavor

Not Afraid of Flavor

Recipes from Magnolia Grill

BEN & KAREN BARKER

PHOTOGRAPHS BY ANN HAWTHORNE

The University of North Carolina Press

Chapel Hill & London

© 2000 Ben and Karen Barker

All rights reserved

Designed by Richard Hendel & Eric M. Brooks

Set in Monotype Garamond by Eric M. Brooks

Frontispiece photograph with the assistance of Gabriel Barker

Printed in Hong Kong by C & C Offset Printing Co., Ltd.

The paper in this book meets the guidelines for permanence
and durability of the Committee on Production Guidelines for
Book Longevity of the Council on Library Resources.

Library of Congress Cataloging-in-Publication Data

Barker, Ben.

Not afraid of flavor: recipes from Magnolia Grill /
by Ben and Karen Barker.

　p.　cm.

Includes index.

ISBN 0-8078-2585-9 (cloth: alk. paper)

1. Cookery, American.　I. Barker, Karen.　II. Magnolia Grill.
III. Title.

TX715.B254　2000

641.5973—dc21　　00-029900

04　03　02　01　　　5　4　3　2

For G. and A.

contents

Preface

What possesses two people to want to open a restaurant?

We sat next to each other on our first day of class at the Culinary Institute of America. Within weeks, without fully realizing it, we had embarked on the journey that has enabled us to share our passion, *our passions*, our craft, and our lives in an often time- and labor-intensive fashion. The paths each of us had followed to our meeting that day were very different, yet as our relationship grew, we gained a shared purpose that defined our culinary education. Throughout the program at CIA, we sought to extract as much knowledge as we possibly could to prepare ourselves for the restaurant we would one day create. It was a wildly romantic, monumentally stimulating time; we were learning many things about technique, ingredients, culinary history, and the foundations of contemporary cuisine. When we weren't in class, or working in restaurants, we were cooking, tasting wine, and devouring any piece of reading material about food that we could lay our hands on. And we were in love.

After graduation, in 1981, we separated to begin new jobs: Karen in Nantucket and Ben in Charlotte, North Carolina. Six months later, we were married, and shortly thereafter, we were reunited in the kitchen, at Restaurant La Residence in Chapel Hill, North Carolina. Founded by Bill and Moreton Neal, "La Rez" represented the model for the restaurant we hoped to open one day: chef-owned, kitchen-driven, with an all-consuming dedication to a seasonal, ever-changing and evolving menu. We arrived in a kitchen from which Bill Neal had recently departed, leaving a crew of wonderful disciples intent on preserving his legacy. It was a dramatic and heady period for us as cooks. With little experience in the fine dining arena, we learned Bill's recipes, his food sensibilities, and, most important, his absolute integrity in all aspects of food preparation, sourcing of ingredients, and cultivation of the supplier relationship. We brought a different orientation to the mix and soon began to influence the menu with our own ideas. Many days brought menu genesis at its most romantic level: we have these ingredients; what can we make with them? Experimentation ran rampant; we read cookbooks voraciously and then descended on the kitchen like Huns sweeping across the steppes, eager to test our skills on unsuspecting customers. As long as we could call our new dishes something in French, there were no boundaries. Many of these creations were successful; some were abysmal failures.

After nearly two years at La Residence, we began to look for other opportunities to expand our roles and responsibilities. La Rez had moved into Chapel Hill when the original site of the restaurant, in rural Chatham County, was restructured by Jenny and R. B. Fitch—as part of their development of the surrounding pasture-lands as the Village of Fearrington—into the Fearrington House. Embodying the Fitches' vision, the restaurant was situated in the rambling old farmhouse that had been home to La Residence, now freshly renovated and redecorated. National acclaim had touched the restaurant under the direction of the great Edna Lewis, the

country's leading exponent of high Southern cuisine, seasonal ingredients, and indigenous producers. When Miss Edna returned to New York, the kitchen staff at Fearrington continued to act in her stead, but it seemed to us that the situation presented an opportunity for us as a chef-couple to make an impact and proceed further along the learning curve we were on. We presented ourselves to the Fitches as candidates endowed with the abilities to create, as R. B. termed it, "the cuisine of the New South"—and the Fitches gave us the job. They invested considerable faith in us, given our limited credentials, and it was occasionally a rocky road. Not only were we thrust into the limelight as the originators of the menu, but our untested capabilities for creating and managing a staff, developing an all-American wine list, and supervising an established operation were all on the line.

The challenge of working within the Southern idiom loomed large on its own. Presented with the opportunity to develop our own style, we chose to follow the guidance of Bill Neal in our neck of the woods and Alice Waters in California by cultivating a network of suppliers, growers, and purveyors who could determine the path of the menu. Adopting the mantra "ingredient-driven cuisine," we set off on a labor-intensive search for local growers at our still-nascent farmers' market, for suppliers of old-fashioned indigenous ingredients like stone-ground cornmeal and flours from Lindley Mills in Alamance County, and for small seafood brokers from the North Carolina coast willing to drive three and a half hours to bring us better quality fish and shellfish.

The Fitches gave us an extraordinary environment to work in, with herb gardens right outside the kitchen door, free rein with the menu (after a time), and a developed clientele stimulated by our excitement over the food we were creating. We learned so much about ourselves, our limitations and our potential, that when the owners of a small health food grocery store in Durham moved to larger quarters and offered us their former space, we felt the timing was right for us to open a restaurant of our own.

The exact moment when we realized that, barely four years out of culinary school, we were going to realize our dream is lost to us now. Many people were of the opinion that opening a fine dining establishment on the periphery of West Durham's business district was suicidal. No evidence existed to show demand for the type of restaurant we proposed to have in the little brick building on the corner of Ninth and Knox. And yet, we knew that if we pursued great ingredients, prepared them with adroitness and passion, and invested ourselves in the success of our staff, we couldn't help but achieve our goals.

Since we opened Magnolia Grill in November 1986, an extraordinary array of folks have passed through our doors, both front and back. If it weren't for the dedication, skills, and integrity of all those coming in the back door, we would never have had so many walk through the front. We have taught, learned, made mistakes, burned pots and bridges, and, we hope, grown as chefs and as people. We have observed proudly a number of young people pass through our kitchen en route to their own dreams of running or owning a restaurant.

This book represents a testimonial of sorts to the guests and staff who have enabled us to continue to live our dream. Of course, there have been days when circumstances have coincided to cause us to question our choice of direction. Even so, on the not-so-infrequent evenings when everyone in the kitchen is clicking and the plates of fearless food exit gorgeous and well-executed to an appreciative (and often noisy) audience, we're reminded of the days when we first set out on this road. And the question is answered: after twenty years of cooking together, we're still in love with what we do and we're still in love. And we still believe, as Henry David Thoreau said, "To affect the quality of the day, that is the highest of the arts."

Acknowledgments

Many chefs have mentors: individuals who, through the power of their knowledge, experience, and personality, determine the conceptualization and style that define a chef's career. We came from culinary school to a region that offered limited opportunities for finding a mentor. Fortunately, the region was home to Bill Neal, who was ahead of his time as a chef, proprietor, and teacher. We are here because he gave us the confidence to be. Our only regret is that we were not able to cook with him. To our mentors in absentia—chefs and cookbook authors whose words we devoured and learned from, such as Madeleine Kamman, Paula Wolfert, Jasper White, Damon Lee Fowler, John Martin Taylor, and Maida Heatter—our debt is immeasurable.

Thanks are also due to many other people:

To all the cooks, bakers, and front-of-the-house folks at Magnolia Grill, all the farmers we depend on, and all the friends of the restaurant.

To our families (particularly the bubbies and grandmothers) for memories and inspirations.

To the UNC Press for giving us a great deal of freedom in doing this book. To Ron Maner for the fearless editing, Rich Hendel for the great design, and David Perry for keeping the book close to home.

To Ann Hawthorne, who was a joy to work with on the photography.

To Rick Robinson, who was the first to give our food the "not afraid of flavor" description.

To Jean Anderson, who has always been incredibly generous with her knowledge of the publishing world and support of the restaurant.

To Frank Stitt and Bob Kinkead, whose restaurants we've always admired and whose friendships we're fortunate to have, and to Louis and Marlene Osteen for bringing us all together.

To Joel Fleishman, our patron saint, for including us in those fortunate to be his friend.

To LizBeth Videau, who helped initiate this project.

And to Tammy Carwane, who organizes our restaurant and our lives, puts up with us on a daily basis, and was invaluable in putting this book together.

Not
Afraid
of
Flavor

Introduction

There is very little pretense to Magnolia Grill. Housed in a flat-roofed brick building on the periphery of an old residential area in one direction and an active business district in the other, it most resembles a truck stop of a "certain" age. We have always loved the contrast in image this creates: relaxed, a bit offbeat, lacking in some of the accoutrements usually considered typical of fine dining establishments (crystal, silver, fine china). Designed on a shoestring budget, the interior of the Grill has not changed much over the years. While paint and new upholstery freshen things up periodically, we've maintained the simple feeling of a breezy, open veranda. We are a neighborhood bistro whose neighborhood has grown.

The history of our building has always been linked to food. Originally constructed as a small independent grocery store, it was utilized for that purpose for the bulk of its existence until it became our restaurant in 1986. That link has ultimately driven our approach to the food we prepare and the style of business we operate.

The Grill is a mom-and-pop operation; we continue to be very hands-on about running the restaurant. Over the years, our menu has grown in complexity, and we now serve more people in an evening than we once imagined possible. The restaurant continues to evolve, but our goal has remained constant—to feature food we love complemented by wonderful wine in a gracious and welcoming atmosphere. We've always been very fortunate in having an incredible staff that executes this vision. It takes a great deal of dedication, attention to detail, and hard work to achieve this. Distinctive restaurants have their own personalities, and we've always felt that the Magnolia "family" is the real soul of our restaurant.

People are always asking us to categorize our food. In response, we've found it difficult to reduce what we do to a three-word sound bite. We look for ingredients that are innately good and seek to present them in ways that accentuate their good qualities. Our presentations are generally straightforward, reveling in the look of the food itself and how it tastes. Our motto, "not afraid of flavor," is typified by dishes that are bold and exciting, often featuring layers of flavors, contrasts in temperature, and textural foils, with honest, gutsy appeal. If something is "not afraid," one can definitely taste all the advertised flavors, but the dish will taste balanced. It will remain interesting to eat from the first bite to the last. Our cooking has principally been based on regional ingredients of the best quality; while not always intrinsically Southern, our cuisine bespeaks a Southern sensibility. While we've never had "specials" or "signature dishes," thematic representations reappear as the seasonal ebb and flow dictates the evolution of our cooking.

If there has been a single defining influence on our cooking, it has been the ingredients we use and our interaction with the network of growers from whom we get them. Our local farmers' market in Carrboro has been a wonderful source of inspiration, renewal, emphatic delineation of the seasonal cadence, and—not least—enduring friendships. Since its inception nearly twenty years ago, the market and the number of vendors selling there have grown; the requirement that all growers

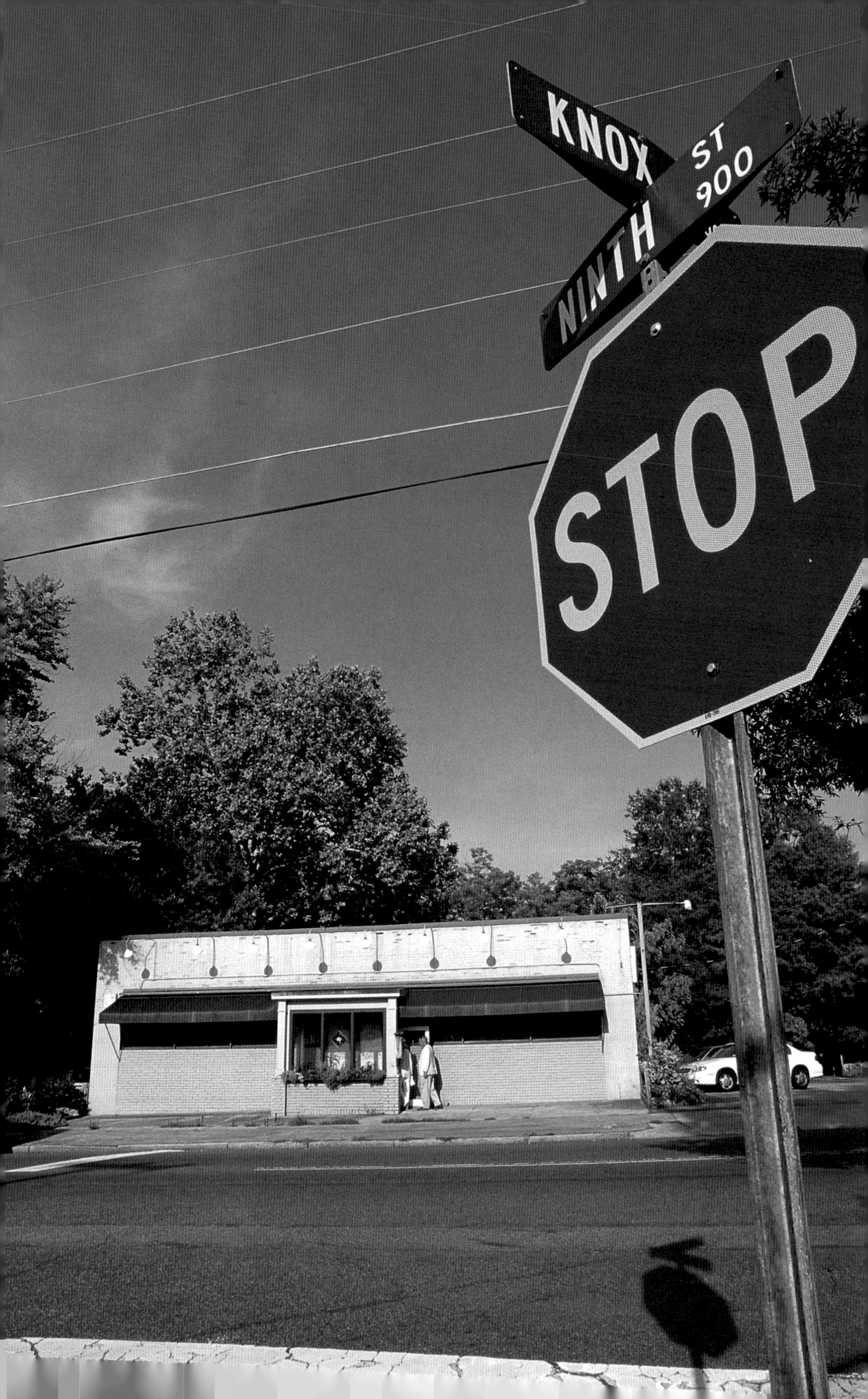
KNOX
NINTH
ST
900
STOP

be from within a fifty-mile radius of the market and sell only what they themselves have produced gives it a distinct regional feel.

If you have a local farmers' market, use it to your advantage. Go early for the best selection. Make an initial walk-through to see what catches your eye, and then let the ingredients create your menu, in the most spontaneous sense. You'll find varieties of vegetables not available in a traditional supermarket, grown for their flavor and not for their ability to be shipped long distances. There is an extraordinary immediacy to food that is grown and picked for you, an opportunity to interact with the farmer that integrates you into the process of bringing the food to the table. Once you employ this approach in your shopping, you'll find you have greater command of your meal planning. Purchasing based on the quality and appeal of the ingredients will yield more gratifying end results and a more natural, satisfying style of cooking.

We cannot overemphasize the importance of using the finest ingredients available to you. Sometimes the difference between a home rendering of a restaurant's recipe and the professional's version is not in the skill of the cook but in the quality of the ingredients. We spend a great deal of time securing the food upon which our menu is based. Just as we have worked to develop ongoing relationships with all our suppliers, you should get to know your local butcher, wine purveyor, fishmonger, and cheese specialist as well. In restaurant lingo, if you are a regular customer, they will "hook you up"—meaning you'll be more likely to receive a superior product, good advice, and excellent service.

When we set out to write this book, the biggest quandary we faced was the issue of whether we should simplify the recipes for home use or present them in true restaurant format. Most of the food served at Magnolia Grill is not innately simple. A desired flavor profile is usually built on a layering of tastes, temperatures, and textures. In a restaurant kitchen, dishes are often broken into components, and the bulk of the actual preparation is done ahead of time. A dish is completed and individually assembled when ordered. Akin to a well-choreographed ballet, this sequence occurs day in and day out at the Grill, but it can doubtless seem a bit daunting to the home cook.

Gladys Scarborough, former owner of the building that is home to Magnolia Grill.

After careful consideration, we have chosen to provide readers with our recipes formatted to home kitchen proportions. We felt that to do anything less would disappoint customers who have eaten our food and are interested in replicating it for themselves. Each plate at Magnolia Grill comes fully garnished, and many of our dishes do require a fair amount of preparation. But logical adjustments can be made for home preparation. If you desire, you can spread the preliminary preparation steps in a number of the recipes out over several days. It is certainly feasible to simplify many recipes by forgoing side accompaniments. An entrée can be rounded out with a green salad. We tend to cook with a fair number of ingredients. This results in dishes that have several nuances and, yes, a lot of flavor. But, coupled with the fact that we have tried to provide the reader with detailed step-by-step directions, it also results in many recipes being lengthy. This does not, however, mean that they are difficult to execute. We hope that you will use these recipes as building blocks to achieve results that please *you*. Feel free to modify the recipes to meet your needs.

You will be most successful with the recipes presented here if you carefully read the recipe all the way through before you start cooking or baking. Prepare a *mise en place*—a culinary term that basically means having all your equipment and ingredients organized and at hand.

One of the most challenging aspects of dealing with food as a medium is that it is rarely exactly the same. The age of an ingredient, the pungency of a spice, the water content of a particular vegetable—all these factors, and more, can affect the product and therefore the outcome of a given dish. It is often difficult to duplicate a recipe without making seasoning or consistency adjustments. Most recipes have a finishing step that instructs you to season to taste. This necessitates that you taste the dish and adjust the quantity of salt, pepper, acidity, and herbs to your liking. Sometimes all a dish needs to bring it together is a bit of salt or a grating of lemon zest. We suggest seasoning gradually, tasting as you go. Refining and training your palate is an ongoing process, and everyone has a different set of likes and dislikes when it comes to food.

A few more things about our recipes and how we hope you'll use them . . .

All eggs are graded large.
All flour, unless otherwise noted, is unbleached all-purpose.
All butter is unsalted.
Cook with all your senses—it's not a strictly literal process.
All citrus juices should be freshly squeezed and strained
   (no plastic lemons, please).
Cook from the heart—it makes a difference.
All salt is kosher salt, except in the dessert recipes,
   which use iodized table salt.
Remember the wise words of the late Lucio Sorré:
   "Food without wine is like walking around naked."
And, above all,
Don't be afraid of flavor!

tar heel tapas, dixie delights, & a few cocktails

Southern-Style Spicy Pecans

Baby Butterbean Crostini

Caramelized Vidalia Onion
    & Bacon Crostata

Cheese Straws

Cheddar Linzers with Hot Pepper Jelly

Barbecued Smoked Salmon with Piccalilli
    & Buttermilk Herb Crackers

Green Olive, Country Ham,
    & Gruyère Fritters

Smoked Pork Tenderloin Angel Biscuits
    with Green Tomato Butter

Okra Rellenos

Deviled Eggs with Caviar

Blackberry Vodka Tonics

Peach Fuzzbusters

Pineapple Ginger Fizz

Watermelon Margranita

Southern-Style Spicy Pecans

These nuts make wonderful cocktail nibbles and can also be used as an interesting garnish on green salads.

INGREDIENTS

    2 egg whites

    1½ teaspoons salt

    ½ cup sugar

    1 tablespoon cayenne pepper

    2 tablespoons sweet paprika

    2 teaspoons Worcestershire sauce

    4½ cups pecan halves

PREPARATION

1. Preheat oven to 350°.
2. In a large stainless steel bowl, whisk the egg whites till foamy. Whisk in the salt and gradually add the sugar, beating the egg whites to stiff peaks. Add the cayenne, paprika, and Worcestershire sauce and whisk to combine.
3. Using a spatula, fold in the pecan halves, making sure to coat them evenly with the egg white mixture. Turn the nuts out onto a nonstick baking pan or Silpat-lined baking sheet, arranging them in single layer. (See note.)
4. Bake the nuts for 5 minutes. Remove from the oven and, using a metal spatula, turn them over, breaking up any large clumps. Return the nuts to the oven and bake an additional 5 minutes. Repeat the process, stirring and turning the nuts every few minutes until they are dry and evenly browned. Remove from the oven, separate into single pecan halves, and allow to cool. Store in an airtight container for up to 5 days.

Note: These crunchy nuts tend to stick to baking sheets, making cleanup a mess. We recommend using a Silpat, or baker's, sheet. The nonstick, flexible silicone-coated pan liner is reusable and easily cleanable. You can find these baking wonders in many specialty kitchenware supply shops (see Sources).

The spiciness of these nuts is dependent on the strength and freshness of the cayenne pepper. The amount called for yields a mild to medium-spiced nut. For extra kick, increase the amount of cayenne.

Baby Butterbean Crostini

The word "butterbean" is best pronounced with a distinct Southern drawl. Butterbeans are kin to the stodgy lima but are much smaller, sweeter, and devoid of the nasty connotation that limas have for many people.

INGREDIENTS FOR THE BUTTERBEAN PURÉE

2 tablespoons olive oil

¼ cup sliced shallots

1 bay leaf, preferably fresh

8 ounces butterbeans, fresh or frozen

approximately 1¾ cups vegetable or chicken stock (or enough to cover beans)

2 tablespoons roasted garlic purée (page 245)

zest of 2 lemons, grated

2 tablespoons extra virgin olive oil

salt and freshly ground black pepper to taste

¼ cup herbs of your choice, chopped (we like a mixture of marjoram, Italian parsley, and basil)

INGREDIENTS FOR COMPLETING THE CROSTINI

1 loaf French-style baguette bread, sliced ½ inch thick on a slight bias

¼ cup olive oil

additional herbs for garnishing

PREPARATION

1. Heat 2 tablespoons of olive oil in a medium sauté pan. Add the sliced shallots and the bay leaf. Sauté the shallots till soft. Add the butterbeans and enough stock to just cover them. Bring to a simmer, reduce the heat, and cook till the beans are tender, adding a bit more stock if necessary. Cool completely over an ice bath. Remove the bay leaf.

2. Rough purée the butterbeans in a food processor, pulsing. *Do not overprocess—* they should retain a bit of texture. Add the roasted garlic purée, lemon zest, extra virgin olive oil, salt and black pepper, and herbs. Pulse to combine. Refrigerate if not using immediately. Bring to room temperature before assembling the crostini. This is best made shortly before using, as the color has a tendency to turn if prepared too far in advance.

3. To assemble the crostini, brush the baguette slices with olive oil on both sides. Grill or toast the bread till golden brown. Slather it generously with butterbean purée and sprinkle with additional herbs.

Caramelized Vidalia Onion & Bacon Crostata

MAKES 1 12-INCH CROSTATA

This rich, flaky rustic tart dough is very versatile and can be used for both sweet and savory dishes. With crostatas, as with pizzas, the flavor variations are endless. Small slices make a wonderful hors d'oeuvre, and a larger piece, combined with a salad, can easily serve as an appetizer or luncheon entrée.

CRUST INGREDIENTS

- 2 cups flour
- 1 teaspoon sugar
- ½ teaspoon salt
- 8 ounces butter, chilled, cut into pieces
- approximately ⅜ cup cold water

FILLING INGREDIENTS

- 10 strips bacon
- 2 tablespoons olive oil
- 4 large Vidalia onions, peeled, cut in half, and sliced thin
- 6 cloves garlic, finely chopped
- 3 tablespoons fresh thyme, divided
- 2 tablespoons fresh chopped parsley, divided
- salt and freshly ground black pepper
- ¼ cup grated Parmesan cheese, divided
- 1 tablespoon olive oil

CRUST PREPARATION

1. In a processor with a steel blade, combine the flour, sugar, and salt. Pulse briefly.
2. Add the butter and pulse to cut in until the mixture resembles coarse meal.
3. Add enough water, pulsing, so that the dough *just* starts to come together. Do not overprocess! Gather the dough together, flatten, wrap in plastic, and chill for several hours. Meanwhile, prepare the filling.

FILLING PREPARATION

1. Stack the bacon strips and cut crosswise, ½ inch thick. Place in a large skillet and cook over medium heat, stirring occasionally, until the bacon is rendered and crisp. Remove the bacon, drain on a paper towel, and reserve.
2. Remove excess bacon fat from the pan and add 2 tablespoons olive oil. Heat the oil and add the onions. Stir and cover the skillet with a lid or foil. Cook the onions over low heat, stirring occasionally, until soft. Add the garlic and cook, covered, for an additional 4 to 5 minutes.
3. Remove the lid, raise the heat to medium, and cook, stirring, until the onions are golden and lightly caramelized. Remove from the heat and stir in the bacon, 2 tablespoons thyme, and 1 tablespoon chopped parsley (reserve the remaining

herbs), and season to taste with salt and black pepper. Allow the onion mixture to cool thoroughly.

4. Preheat oven to 375°.
5. On a lightly floured surface, roll the pastry out into a circle approximately 16 inches in diameter and ⅛ inch thick. Place on a parchment paper–lined baking sheet.
6. Sprinkle the pastry with 2 tablespoons of Parmesan cheese. Leaving a ¾-inch border around the outside edge, spread the onion mixture evenly over the surface of the dough. Sprinkle the remaining Parmesan cheese over the onions. Drizzle with 1 tablespoon olive oil.
7. Fold the border up over the onion filling, pleating as necessary, to form a rustic-looking tart.
8. Bake for approximately 35 minutes, until the pastry is golden brown. Remove from the oven and sprinkle with the remaining chopped herbs. Serve warm or at room temperature.

Cheese Straws

MAKES APPROXIMATELY 3 DOZEN

These simple, light-as-a-feather cheese straws need no further adornment—they are a hit at every party when we serve them. While they can be made with frozen prepared puff pastry, using your own "quickie puff pastry" is really preferable. This recipe produces a very flaky, delicate pastry and is infinitely faster and less exacting than the traditional French method.

INGREDIENTS FOR THE PUFF PASTRY
    2 cups flour
    1 teaspoon salt
    3¼ sticks butter (26 tablespoons), chilled and cut into small pieces
    ½ cup cold water

INGREDIENTS FOR THE CHEESE STRAWS
    1 egg
    ¼ teaspoon water
    1½ cups finely grated Parmesan cheese (we grate ours in a processor with a
        steel blade)
    ⅜ teaspoon cayenne pepper
    1 teaspoon paprika

PREPARATION FOR THE PUFF PASTRY
    1. Combine the flour, salt, and butter in a mixer bowl and mix, on low speed, using a paddle, until the butter breaks up slightly (about 1 minute). Add the water and mix until the mixture just barely comes together. Do not overwork! This can also be done in a food processor, using the pulse mechanism.

2. Gather the dough mass into a rectangular shape and place on a lightly floured surface. Using a lightly floured rolling pin, roll the dough into a 12 × 7-inch rectangle. Fold into thirds lengthwise, as if you were folding a letter. Give the dough package a quarter turn to the right, lightly reflour the working surface and the top of the dough, and roll the dough out again. Fold the dough into thirds, give it a quarter turn, and repeat this same rolling/folding process 2 more times, for a total of 4 "turns." Wrap the dough in plastic and refrigerate for 2 hours. Remove from the refrigerator for 10 minutes and repeat the rolling/folding process 2 additional times, for a total of 6 "turns." Rewrap the dough in plastic and chill 2 hours before using. This dough can be made ahead and frozen for up to 2 months or refrigerated for up to 3 days. If you have frozen the dough, allow it to defrost in the refrigerator overnight. Always remove the dough from the refrigerator about 10 to 15 minutes before rolling out the cheese straws.

PREPARATION FOR THE CHEESE STRAWS

1. Place the egg and water in a small bowl and beat to combine. Reserve.
2. Combine the Parmesan, cayenne, and paprika and mix well. Reserve.
3. On a lightly floured surface, roll the puff pastry out into a 9 × 16-inch rectangle. Brush the top of the dough with some of the egg wash and sprinkle evenly with half of the cheese mixture. With a lightly floured rolling pin, press the cheese into the dough, using a light rolling motion. Turn the dough over and repeat the egg wash, cheese sprinkling, and rolling process.
4. Trim the edges of the dough—a pizza wheel is the ideal tool to accomplish this. Cut the dough in half lengthwise and then cut crosswise into ¾-inch-thick sticks.
5. Line baking sheets with parchment paper and sprinkle the parchment lightly with flour.
6. Pick the cheese straws up, holding both ends, and gently stretch and twist them before placing them on the prepared baking sheet. Leave 1½ inches between each straw. Place the cheese straws in the refrigerator or freezer and chill till very firm. They can be made ahead to this point and frozen.
7. Bake in a preheated oven at 425° for 12 minutes, until the cheese straws are well "puffed." Turn the baking sheet around. Turn the oven to 325° and bake for an additional 15 to 18 minutes, until the cheese straws are starting to brown lightly. Remove from the oven and allow to cool for 2 to 3 minutes. With a metal spatula or pie server, remove the cheese straws from the baking sheet while still warm. Allow to cool.
8. Serve within 1 hour. You can bake these in advance and recrisp them shortly before serving.

Cheddar Linzers with Hot Pepper Jelly

YIELDS 4 DOZEN

Ben's mother, Jeanette Barker, is an amazing hostess, and our cheddar linzers were inspired by her recipe for thumbprints, which uses the same basic dough in a different presentation. We think the faux linzer format is a bit more playful. People will wonder why a cookie has made its way into an hors d'oeuvre selection and will be surprised by its savory nature. While homemade hot pepper jelly can certainly be used, there are a number of good commercial varieties available. We recommend the one made by American Spoon Foods (see Sources)—their entire product line is simply wonderful.

INGREDIENTS

> 4 ounces butter, at room temperature
> 1 pound sharp orange cheddar cheese, grated
> ½ teaspoon salt
> ¼ teaspoon Tabasco
> ¼ teaspoon cayenne pepper
> ¼ teaspoon dry mustard
> 1½ cups flour
> 1 jar hot pepper jelly

PREPARATION

1. Preheat oven to 350°.
2. Cream the butter till soft. Add the cheddar cheese. Add the salt, Tabasco, cayenne, and mustard. Gradually add the flour and blend in. The mixture will be fairly stiff. Divide the dough in half and work with one piece at a time.
3. On a lightly floured surface, roll the dough out to a thickness of ⅛ inch. Using a 2-inch round cutter, cut rounds in the dough. Using a ½-inch cutter, cut small circles in the center of half of the 2-inch rounds. Place the cut-out rounds on a parchment lined baking sheet. Reform the dough and cut once more. Discard the remaining scraps.
4. Bake approximately 15 minutes, until the pastry is lightly golden. Cool completely. These can be baked up to 24 hours in advance. If making ahead, store in an airtight container before filling.
5. To fill, turn the plain circles over and place a generous dab of hot pepper jelly in the center of each round. Top with a round that has a cut-out center. The linzers can be filled up to 1½ hours before serving.

Barbecued Smoked Salmon with Piccalilli & Buttermilk Herb Crackers

SERVES A PILE OF FOLKS

You may serve the salmon as a component of several hors d'oeuvres or as a first course with a small salad. If you wish, you may substitute commercial relish or a tangy green tomato chutney for the piccalilli. Leftover salmon can be tossed with a simple pasta, used for an extra zippy morning bagel, or stirred into soft scrambled eggs.

Given its large yield, this recipe is one to try for a big gathering as opposed to a small, intimate dinner. Note that the recipe is prepared over a period of several days and requires advance planning. Leftovers will keep for several days if well wrapped.

The process of curing and cold-smoking your own salmon is not difficult and is particularly feasible if you own a smoker or a covered kettle grill. Stove-top cold-smokers can also be used. See page 89 for tips on smoking.

INGREDIENTS FOR THE SALMON

1 side salmon filet, skin on, pin bones removed (approximately 2–2 ½ pounds)

INGREDIENTS FOR THE BRINE

½ cup brown sugar

2 ¾ tablespoons white sugar

½ cup + ⅓ cup kosher salt

8 cups water

1 cup cider

¼ cup crushed red pepper flakes

¼ cup paprika

⅛ cup black peppercorns, coarsely crushed

¼ cup coriander seeds, coarsely crushed

¼ cup mustard seeds, coarsely crushed

4 bay leaves, preferably fresh

1 medium onion, peeled and sliced thin

INGREDIENTS FOR THE RUB

¼ cup paprika

⅛ cup cayenne pepper

1 tablespoon crushed red pepper flakes

1 tablespoon crushed black peppercorns

1 tablespoon coriander seeds, crushed

1 tablespoon mustard seeds, ground

¼ cup chopped parsley, preferably flat-leaf

⅛ cup lemon thyme leaves

1 cup cider (as needed)

INGREDIENTS FOR SERVING

1 recipe buttermilk herb crackers (page 174)

1 recipe piccalilli (page 178)

1. Combine all of the brine ingredients in a nonreactive saucepot. Bring to a boil. Cool, then chill completely.
2. Place the salmon filet and chilled brine in a deep nonreactive pan. Stir to distribute the ingredients. Cover and refrigerate for 36 hours.
3. Remove the salmon from the brine, pat dry, and place on a rack situated over a baking pan. Refrigerate uncovered for 24 hours to allow a "skin" to form. This "skin," called the pellicle, enhances the absorption of the smoke as well as the aesthetic appearance.
4. Combine all of the dry ingredients listed for the rub. Add enough cider to make a dry paste. Spread the paste on all surfaces of the salmon filet except the natural skin.
5. Cold-smoke the salmon filet over apple and hickory for 30 minutes.
6. Chill completely. Slice paper-thin and serve immediately on buttermilk herb crackers topped with piccalilli.

Note: You may substitute thin-sliced black bread for the buttermilk herb crackers if you wish.

Green Olive, Country Ham, & Gruyère Fritters

MAKES ABOUT 75

Fondly known in the Magnolia Grill kitchen as cheese balls, these crispy treats can be quite addictive.

INGREDIENTS

6 eggs, separated, whites reserved
¾ cup milk
1½ cups flour
1½ pounds Gruyère, grated
½ cup cooked country ham, minced fine
⅓ cup grated Parmesan cheese
½ cup pitted green olives, minced fine
1 tablespoon finely chopped garlic
salt and freshly ground black pepper
Tabasco
2 tablespoons chopped fresh Italian parsley
peanut oil for frying

PREPARATION

1. Beat the egg yolks with a whisk until lemon-colored. Stir in the milk, then gradually add the flour and beat until smooth. Using a rubber spatula, fold in all the remaining ingredients except the egg whites.
2. Beat the egg whites until stiff but not dry. Fold the yolk mixture into the whites.

3. Heat oil in an electric skillet or deep, heavy pot to 350° (use a deep-frying thermometer).
4. Drop the batter into the oil by spoonfuls and cook, turning once if necessary, until golden. Fry in batches.
5. Drain and serve immediately.

Smoked Pork Tenderloin Angel Biscuits with Green Tomato Butter

APPROXIMATELY 3 DOZEN

This hors d'oeuvre is a variation on traditional ham biscuits—a staple that is often found at Southern family reunions, wedding receptions, and local breakfast grills. This recipe also works well with thin-sliced country ham or a simple roasted pork tenderloin. You may also serve the biscuits with prepared chutney and/or mustard if you wish to omit the green tomato butter.

INGREDIENTS
    1 recipe smoked pork tenderloin (page 88)
    1 recipe angel biscuits (page 176)
    1 recipe green tomato butter (page 177)

TO ASSEMBLE THE BISCUITS
    Warm the angel biscuits lightly if they were baked ahead of time. Split them with a serrated knife and spread with green tomato butter. Fill with sliced pork loin and serve.

Okra Rellenos

MAKES ABOUT 3 DOZEN

These are given a Southern slant with their filling of old-fashioned pimiento cheese—which is a wonderful recipe by itself. Grilled cheese sandwiches filled with this spread and cut into quarters is another, less labor-intensive hors d'oeuvre idea. We do think that if you have the time, these rellenos are worth the effort. Please note that we endorse the idea of using prepared Talk o' Texas brand okra pickles. They are terrific, and we've never found a recipe for making your own that yielded a better product. We also use Duke's prepared mayonnaise in this recipe. Available in the Southern market but not nationwide, in our opinion it's the best commercial mayonnaise there is.

INGREDIENTS FOR THE PIMIENTO CHEESE
    12 ounces sharp orange cheddar cheese, grated
    scant ½ cup mayonnaise
    ½ cup jarred pimientos, drained and chopped fine
    1 teaspoon Worcestershire sauce

½ teaspoon Tabasco

½ teaspoon dry mustard

salt and freshly ground black pepper to taste

INGREDIENTS FOR THE RELLENOS

2 16-ounce jars Talk o' Texas okra pickles (hot or mild)

3 eggs

2 cups flour, divided

1 ½ cups yellow stone-ground cornmeal

salt and freshly ground black pepper

peanut oil for frying

PREPARATION FOR THE PIMIENTO CHEESE

1. Place all the ingredients except the salt and pepper in a bowl and stir together till well combined.

2. Season the pimiento cheese with salt and black pepper to taste. Can be made up to 2 days ahead. Store covered in the refrigerator if not using immediately.

PREPARATION FOR THE RELLENOS

1. Drain the okra pickles well and place them on paper towels to dry. Using a paring knife, slit one pickle lengthwise from just below the cap three-quarters of the way down, taking care not to cut through the opposite side. Gently remove most of the seeds and ribs from the interior. Repeat with the remaining okra pods.

2. Fill each okra cavity with pimiento cheese mixture, using a spoon or a small pastry bag. Place the stuffed okra pickles in the refrigerator while you prepare the breading. Chill thoroughly.

3. Whisk the eggs in a bowl to combine well. Reserve. Place 1 ½ cups flour in another bowl or shallow pie pan. Combine the remaining ½ cup flour with the cornmeal in a third bowl or pie pan. Season the flour-cornmeal mixture with salt and black pepper and mix to combine.

4. Dip each relleno in flour. Shake off the excess and dip the pickle in the egg wash. Let excess egg drain off and then dredge the relleno in the seasoned cornmeal mixture. Place on a platter and allow to dry for 15 to 20 minutes. Redredge in the cornmeal mixture before frying if the rellenos seem at all moist.

5. Pour peanut oil to a depth of ½ inch in a large heavy-bottomed skillet. Heat to approximately 365° and carefully add the rellenos. Do not overcrowd the skillet. Cook, turning once or twice, till golden brown. Remove and drain on paper toweling. Repeat till all the rellenos are fried. Cool slightly before serving.

Deviled Eggs with Caviar

MAKES 2 DOZEN

Otherwise known as "eggs on eggs," this gilded potluck dinner staple was among the hors d'oeuvres that we served at our last James Beard House dinner in New York. As is always the case with deviled eggs, the platters were completely cleaned.

INGREDIENTS

12 large eggs
½ cup mayonnaise (prepared or your own homemade)
2 teaspoons Dijon mustard
½ teaspoon Worcestershire sauce
½ teaspoon Tabasco
2 tablespoons minced chives
salt and freshly ground black pepper to taste
1 ounce sturgeon caviar (best quality American or imported)
finely minced chives as garnish

PREPARATION

1. Place the eggs in a saucepan. Cover with water and bring to a boil. Cover the pan, remove from heat, and allow the eggs to sit for exactly 10 minutes. Drain the eggs and cool under cold running water. Once the eggs have cooled, peel them and slice in half lengthwise.

2. Remove the yolks from the eggs and place them in a mixing bowl. Add the mayonnaise to the yolks and mash with a fork until fairly smooth. Add the Dijon mustard, Worcestershire sauce, Tabasco, and chives. Mix until combined. Season with salt and black pepper to taste.

3. Place the egg yolk mixture into a pastry bag and pipe into the reserved, hollowed-out, hard-cooked whites, mounding slightly. The eggs can be made several hours ahead up to this point. Cover with plastic wrap and refrigerate until ready to serve.

4. Before serving, top each deviled egg with a generous spoonful of caviar and sprinkle with a few chives.

Blackberry Vodka Tonics

MAKES ENOUGH FOR 16 COCKTAILS

The inspiration for blackberry vodka tonics came from a bumper crop of juicy Peregrine Farm blackberries. We always put up a batch at the height of berry-picking season, let it mellow for several months or up to a year, and enjoy this refreshing cocktail at the first sign of summer!

INGREDIENTS

    1 pint blackberries
    1 fifth vodka, 90 proof
    tonic water
    lime wedges for garnish

PREPARATION

1. Rinse the blackberries and place in a quart jar. Add vodka, cover tightly, and let stand at room temperature for 4 days, turning the jar over every day. Transfer the jar to the freezer for at least 2 days (it's best after 30 days) or up to a year.
2. Strain the blackberry vodka into a measuring cup. For each cocktail, fill a tall glass with ice and pour in 1 ½ ounces of vodka. Add tonic and garnish with a lime wedge and a few blackberries.

Peach Fuzzbusters

YIELDS 3 8-OUNCE DRINKS

Ben's dad introduced us to the delights of this cocktail. More than one of these combined with an afternoon of sun and fun can definitely leave you a bit fuzzy.

INGREDIENTS

    6 ounces frozen lemonade concentrate
    4 ounces vodka
    3 ripe peaches, halved and pitted (do not skin!)
    1 ½ cups ice cubes
    mint sprigs for garnish

PREPARATION

Combine all of the ingredients in a blender and purée until smooth. Serve in tall glasses, garnished with mint sprigs. Repeat as necessary.

Pineapple Ginger Fizz

YIELDS 1 TALL SUMMER DAY COOLER

Blenheim (see Sources) is a South Carolina company producing old-fashioned, ginger-spicy ales and beers. If you can find them, they're terrific. If not, look for traditional-style ginger ale.

INGREDIENTS

    2 ounces gold rum
    3 ounces pineapple juice (see note)
    2 ounces Blenheim's ginger beer or ginger ale
    ½ ounce lime juice
    lime wedge for garnish

PREPARATION

    Fill a tall, festive glass with ice. Add all of the ingredients. Stir and garnish with a lime wedge. Find an umbrella to sit under.

Note: We use Loóza pineapple juice from Belgium, which is often available in specialty groceries. It is concentrated, but has no additional sugar added. Other brands of pineapple nectar or juice will also work.

Watermelon Margranita

YIELDS I DRINK

If you need an excuse to make watermelon granita, look no further. This summery con-coction is a favorite at the Chateau Relax-o, our beach house on Topsail Island along the North Carolina coast.

INGREDIENTS

    1 ½ ounces gold tequila
    ½ ounce crème de cassis
    ½ ounce lime juice
    3 ounces watermelon granita (page 212)
    lime slice for garnish

PREPARATION

    Combine the ingredients in a blender, pulse to combine, and serve in a martini glass, salted rim optional. Garnish with a lime slice.

soups

Tomato Soup from the Alentejo

Spicy Green Tomato Soup with Crab
    & Country Ham

Chilled Tomato Essence with Tomato-Basil Jello

Celery-Fennel Chowder with Oysters & Bacon

Cool as a Cucumber Soup with Buttermilk, Dill,
    & Vermouth Shrimp

Cream of Vidalia Onion Soup

Curried Butternut Soup with Shrimp
    & Toasted Coconut

New Orleans Red Bean Soup with Andouille
    & Rice

Moroccan Roasted Eggplant Bisque with
    Grilled Chicken & Minted Yogurt

Summersweet Corn Bisque with Shiitake
    Mushrooms, Bacon, & Truffle Oil

Reflections on Life, Food, Chefs, Kings, & Power

BY SASHA KURTZ, AGE 6, CIRCA 1977

the shef

Onsa ponat,me thor was a shef how warckt for the King. The shef alwas mad soop. But the shef didin't know that the king didin't Like soop. So he cKpt on making soop. Morning aftrnoon and night, then on satrday night aftr dinr the king went to the shef and sed "dont you know I hatesoop"! "I didin't know." "weL you know now. No mor soop". So he mad oringscKips. he didin't LicKe that ethre So he firde him
the end.

Reflections on Life, Food, Chefs, Kings, & Power

BY BEN BARKER, AGE 45, CIRCA 1999

Throughout my professional life, I have loved making soups, and I continue to do so to this day. I am firmly convinced that both the chef and the home cook can create wonderful one-dish meals or entries to a more complex menu with minimal effort. Soups can warm you or refresh you, awaken your senses for the food that is to follow or satisfy all your cravings in one fell swoop (just add salad, bread, and vino).

To achieve success with the recipes that follow, you will find several criteria and a few pieces of simple equipment essential, we believe. Critical to all these recipes (except the tomato essence) is the quality of the stock you use. We of course recommend using homemade stock (see page 227), but if time or predilection prohibits you from doing so, low-sodium commercial alternatives are your best bet. We often will infuse the stock we're using with the trimmings from the soup's components, to generate added depth. This technique is especially useful if your stock lacks character. Great stock is the medium for your message.

Select your ingredients carefully. Without belaboring the obvious, too often soups are a hodgepodge of scraps and misguided attempts to salvage something found lurking in the back right corner of the vegetable bin. Purchase with the same care you direct to your holiday roast, and the ingredients will reward you.

Season with authority. Achieving balance through the addition of salt and pepper, adjusting the acidity with vinegar or citrus juice, and modifying nuance with fresh nutmeg, grated citrus zest, fish sauce, Tabasco, or roasted garlic purée can lead to a finished soup that cascades in layers in your mouth.

There are four pieces of equipment that we require for making soup and all of them should be part of your regular kitchen battery:

1. A heavy-bottomed nonreactive pot, with a lid. Heavy-bottomed so you can cook slowly and evenly over low heat or quickly without burning over high heat. Nonreactive (meaning stainless steel or nonreactive aluminum or lined copper) so high-acid foods or wines won't pick up off-tastes. A lid so you can "sweat" your vegetables (i.e., cook slowly, covered, over low heat).
2. A long-handled wooden spoon. Soups prefer the organic feel of wood; stirring and scraping with a metal spoon scares the cat.
3. A food processor or blender for puréed soups.
4. A food mill. We often use a food mill after we've puréed soups to achieve a silky, fine texture. It removes skins and bits of hard spices, fibrous vegetables become satiny—and you're going to need one to make smooth mashed potatoes anyway. Many better models come with 3 interchangeable blades, but we've used a common Foley food mill at home for 18 years.

Three tomato soups;
one hot, one not, one either.
Red, green, translucent.

Tomato Soup from the Alentejo

SERVES 8

Our good friend Jean Anderson is a noted food and travel writer and an authority on the cuisine of Portugal. On her recommendation, and armed with detailed instructions, we once spent two weeks traveling from Lisbon through the Alentejo and out to the coast. This soup is inspired by versions we encountered in our travels; often the egg was poached right in the broth as it was brought steaming to the table. Rustic, texturally dramatic, and thoroughly satisfying, this soup and a large tumbler of red wine erased the weariness of a hot August day in the Portuguese plains.

INGREDIENTS

6 ounces yellow onion, diced

¼ cup olive oil

¼ cup minced garlic

2 bay leaves

1 teaspoon crushed red pepper flakes (or to taste)

1 tablespoon cumin seed, toasted lightly and crushed in a mortar or ground in a spice mill

1 tablespoon coriander seed, toasted lightly and crushed in a mortar or ground in a spice mill

6 large extra ripe tomatoes (about 4 pounds), cored and cut into large chunks (about 1–1½ inches)

1 cup white wine

1½ cups chicken stock

salt, black pepper, and red wine vinegar to taste

2 cups baguette bread, cut into chunks, tossed in olive oil, and lightly toasted

½ cup Manchego cheese, shaved with a potato peeler

8 poached eggs (see note)

1½ cups cilantro leaves, roughly chopped

extra virgin olive oil

PREPARATION

1. Cook the onion in the olive oil until softened and golden. Add the garlic, bay leaves, red pepper flakes, and ground spices. Cook 2 minutes. Add ⅔ of the tomatoes and cook 5 minutes. Add the wine and stock, bring to a simmer, and cook 10 minutes. Remove the bay leaves and pass through a food mill or strain through a sieve, pressing on the solids.

2. Warm the soup over medium heat; season with salt and pepper, adjust the consistency with stock, and adjust the acidity with red wine vinegar. Divide

the remaining tomatoes, the bread chunks, and the Manchego cheese between 8 flat, shallow soup bowls. Place a poached egg in the center of each bowl.

3. Stir the cilantro into the soup and then ladle hot soup over the eggs into the bowls. Drizzle with extra virgin olive oil and sprinkle with a few cilantro leaves. Serve immediately.

Note: To poach the eggs, heat 2 quarts of water with ½ cup white vinegar. Crack each egg and gently slip the white and yolk into barely simmering water; poach until the whites are set but the yolk is still runny, about 2 minutes. Transfer eggs to service bowls as they are cooked.

Spicy Green Tomato Soup with Crab & Country Ham

SERVES 8

This has become an early fall staple at the restaurant, and it is one of our more requested recipes. We suppose everyone needs another use for all those end-of-season green tomatoes besides frying them.

This soup is equally successful chilled or hot, and you can modify the garnish depending on your preference.

INGREDIENTS
    5 ounces country ham, julienned
    ½ cup vegetable oil
    2 medium onions, peeled and sliced thin
    6 cloves garlic, sliced
    2 jalapeños, stemmed and sliced, with seeds
    4 green Anaheims, stemmed, seeded, and sliced
    2 green pasilla chiles, stemmed, seeded, and sliced
    2 bay leaves
    3½ pounds firm green tomatoes, cored and cut into eighths
    1½ quarts shrimp stock (page 233) or homemade chicken stock
    1 handful fresh basil leaves (about 1 cup)
    3 tablespoons lemon juice
    1½ teaspoons Tabasco (or to taste)
    salt to taste

INGREDIENTS FOR THE GARNISH
    country ham (see above)
    1 pound crabmeat, picked over for shells, or 1 pound peeled, cooked shrimp, cut into ¼-inch pieces
    1 cup sour cream, thinned with 2 tablespoons milk
    1 cup fresh tomato concassé (page 237), combined with ¼ cup capers, chopped
    ½ cup scallions, sliced

1. Cook the ham in the vegetable oil until crisp and golden; drain, reserve the ham, and return the oil to the pot.
2. Cook the onions in the oil over moderate heat until soft but not colored. Add the garlic, jalapeños, Anaheims, pasilla chiles, and bay leaves and cook 5 minutes.
3. Add the tomatoes and stock and bring to a boil. Reduce to a simmer and cook 15 minutes, until the tomatoes soften.
4. Remove the bay leaves, add the basil, and purée in a blender, working in batches.
5. Season with lemon juice, Tabasco, and salt. Cool and reserve.
6. Gently reheat the soup over medium heat and adjust the seasoning. Place crab or shrimp in warm bowls. Ladle the soup into the bowls, and garnish with sour cream, tomato concassé and caper mixture, country ham, and sliced scallions.

Chilled Tomato Essence with Tomato-Basil Jello

SERVES 8

We first heard of the technique for making tomato "water" in 1989. Scott Howell, the second sous chef at Magnolia Grill from 1989 to 1991 and now the chef-owner of Nana's in Durham, was working in New York at the time and would call us to talk about the "hip" food he was seeing. As he related the technique, we were intrigued by the opportunity to utilize the wealth of wonderful tomatoes we get every summer in a unique and different way. It takes a lot of super ripe tomatoes to make this essence, but you can use less than perfect fruit, including those "freaks" from the garden with ugly shoulders and a misshapen appearance.

The jello garnish isn't essential but is an interesting addition visually and texturally. It also will change the minds of people who can't abide the thought of tomato aspic.

This soup is dedicated to the memory of Auburn Isley, our tomato man from 1986 to 1994.

INGREDIENTS FOR THE TOMATO ESSENCE

10 pounds very ripe organic tomatoes, cored, blemishes trimmed, and cut into eighths
1 ½ tablespoons salt
6 cloves garlic, sliced
2 jalapeños, sliced, with seeds
1 cup basil leaves, roughly chopped
2 egg whites
¼ cup rice or champagne vinegar
salt and black pepper to taste

INGREDIENTS FOR THE TOMATO-BASIL JELLO

2 cups clarified tomato water, reserved from preparation of tomato essence
1 envelope gelatin

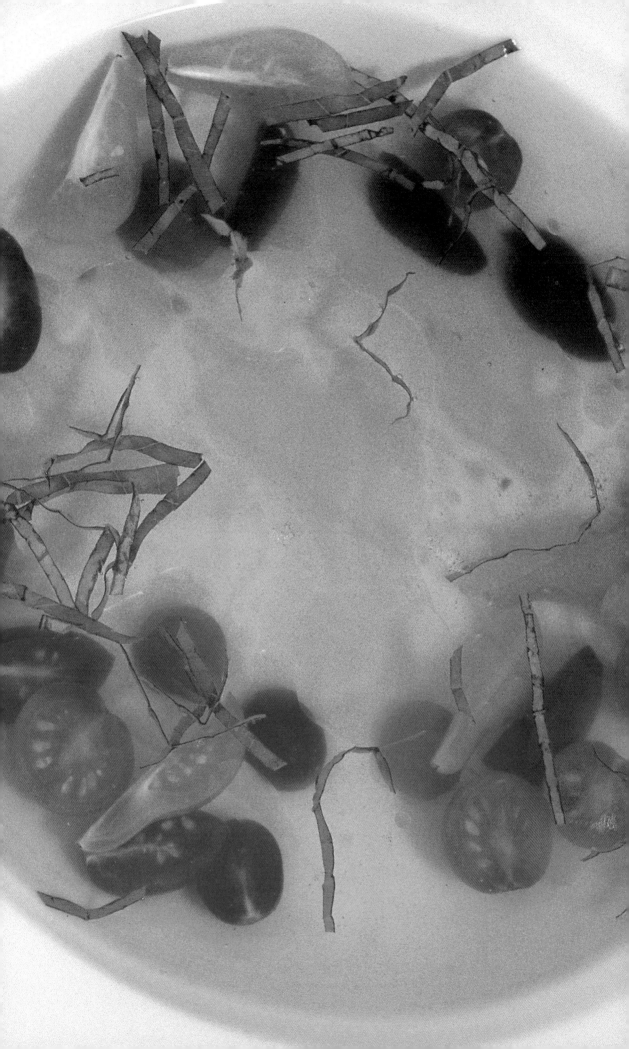

INGREDIENTS FOR THE GARNISH

approximately 2 cups different-colored, ripe cherry tomatoes, cut in half; use
½ cup each of 4 different varieties, choosing among red pear, sweet 100's, and
red currants (red types), sungolds, yellow currants, and yellow pears (yellow
types), and green grapes (a green-ripening type of cherry tomato)

½ cup fresh basil leaves, cut into chiffonade

2–3 tablespoons basil oil (page 240)

PREPARATION FOR THE TOMATO ESSENCE

1. Working in batches if necessary, purée the tomatoes with the salt in a food
   processor. Transfer the purée to a cheesecloth-lined strainer over a container
   and refrigerate overnight.

2. Discard the solids and the cheesecloth. Transfer the tomato "water" to a
   nonreactive pot. Combine the garlic, jalapeños, chopped basil, egg whites,
   vinegar, salt, and pepper in a bowl. Whisk into the "water" and cook over
   medium-high heat, whisking occasionally, until the egg whites begin to
   coagulate. (The soup will look cloudy and bits of pink cooked egg whites will
   float to the top.) Cease whisking, immediately reduce the heat to very low, and
   cook, without stirring, for 10 minutes; the egg white "raft" will congeal and
   clarify the impurities from the soup.

3. Remove from heat. Using a ladle, strain the soup through a clean linen towel or
   double-wrapped cheesecloth into a clean container. Cool and refrigerate to chill
   thoroughly. Season with salt if necessary. Yields about 10 cups, depending on
   the juiciness of the tomatoes. (Reserve 2 cups of the tomato essence for making
   the jello.)

PREPARATION FOR THE TOMATO-BASIL JELLO

1. In a small nonreactive saucepan, warm 1½ cups of the tomato essence over
   medium heat. Combine the remaining ½ cup of essence with the gelatin and
   stir into the warm essence until melted.

2. Remove from heat and pour into a clean, flat container, such as an 8 × 8-inch
   Pyrex dish. Cool, then refrigerate until gelled. Using a paring knife, cut into
   ½-inch squares. Reserve, refrigerated.

TO SERVE

Divide the cherry tomatoes between 8 chilled bowls. Put 1 tablespoon of basil
chiffonade and ¼ cup of diced tomato-basil jello into each bowl. Ladle chilled
essence into each bowl and drizzle a little basil oil to float on top. Serve
immediately.

Celery-Fennel Chowder with Oysters & Bacon

SERVES 8

Oyster chowder may not be truly Southern in origin, fennel bulb was never part of the Barkers' Alamance County larder, and savory sabayon might seem a little foreign—but this is a truly great flavor combination. All the components can be made ahead, but you must not finish the chowder until you are ready to serve it, and then serve it immediately; please don't overpoach the oysters.

If you don't want to fool with the sabayon, a little whipped cream with chopped fennel tops or tarragon folded in is a likely and appropriate alternative.

INGREDIENTS FOR THE CHOWDER BASE

- 4 strips bacon, cut crosswise into julienne
- 2 tablespoons olive oil
- 2 large leeks, trimmed and rinsed
- 2 fennel bulbs (about ¾ pound), tops trimmed, quartered and cored, sliced crosswise ¼ inch thick
- 6 ribs celery, washed and sliced crosswise ¼ inch thick
- ½ cup chopped garlic
- 1½ tablespoons fennel seed, toasted and ground
- pinch crushed red pepper flakes
- 2 bay leaves
- 1½ cups white wine
- ¾ cup oyster liquor (reserved from shucked oysters, see assembly below)
- ¼ cup Pernod or Ricard (anise liquor, optional)
- 3 cups chicken stock

PREPARATION

1. Combine the julienned bacon and olive oil and cook over medium heat until the bacon is rendered and crisp. Remove the bacon to paper toweling to drain, reserving the oil–bacon fat mixture.

2. Split the leeks lengthwise and wash thoroughly to remove sand and grit. Slice crosswise ¼ inch thick. Warm the oil-fat mixture over medium heat and stir in the leeks, fennel, and celery; reduce the heat to medium-low and cover the pan. Cook the vegetables, covered, stirring occasionally, for 10 to 15 minutes, until soft.

3. Add the garlic, fennel seed, red pepper flakes, and bay leaves; cook 2 minutes. Add the wine, oyster liquor (reserved from the oysters that will be added during assembly), and optional Pernod; bring to a boil. Add the chicken stock, bring to a simmer, and cook until the vegetables are tender. Remove from heat, cool slightly, remove the bay leaves, and purée in a blender or food processor. Pass through the fine blade of a food mill if desired. Chill and reserve or continue with the instructions for garnish and assembly.

¼ cup minced fennel green tops or ¼ cup chopped tarragon

¼ pound redskin new potatoes, cut into ½-inch dice

PREPARATION

1. Mince the fennel tops and set aside.

2. Cut the new potatoes into dice. Place in a small saucepot with just enough water to barely cover the potatoes. Add a pinch of salt, bring to a boil, and simmer until tender; drain, then cool in cold water. Drain and reserve.

INGREDIENTS FOR THE OPTIONAL PERNOD SABAYON

2 tablespoons tarragon vinegar

1 tablespoon minced shallot

2 tablespoons white wine

2 tablespoons Pernod or Ricard

1 egg yolk

¼ cup heavy cream

salt

PREPARATION

Combine the vinegar, shallot, wine, and anise liquor in a small saucepan. Bring to a boil; reduce by half, strain, and cool. Combine the reduction and the egg yolk in a double boiler. Whisk over medium heat until thickened and lemon-colored. Remove from heat and let cool. Whip the cream until it forms stiff peaks; fold in the egg mixture and season with salt. Reserve, refrigerated.

INGREDIENTS FOR ASSEMBLY

½ cup half-and-half

tarragon vinegar, grated lemon zest, salt, black pepper, and Tabasco to taste

1 ½ pints shucked oysters, drained (with oyster liquor reserved for chowder)

ASSEMBLY

1. Heat the chowder base over medium-low heat. Stir in the half-and-half, adjust the consistency with additional stock if necessary, and season with tarragon vinegar, grated lemon zest, salt, freshly ground black pepper, and Tabasco to taste.

2. Raise the heat to medium-high. When the chowder just begins to bubble, stir in the drained oysters and cook 1 minute, or until the oysters are barely curled.

3. Divide the potatoes between warm bowls. Divide the oysters into the bowls and then ladle chowder over. Spoon a dollop of sabayon into the center of each and sprinkle with bacon and minced fennel tops. Serve immediately.

Cool as a Cucumber Soup with Buttermilk, Dill, & Vermouth Shrimp

SERVES 8

In the summer, Ben's grandmother would serve lunch on her ceramic tile–floored screened porch. In the shade of old oak trees, sliced German Johnson tomatoes warm from the garden were accompanied by sliced cucumbers and onions in vinegar, cool and crunchy and accentuated by their acidity. This soup is the inverse presentation. It's easy to make—there is virtually no cooking involved—and it's refreshingly invigorating.

INGREDIENTS

3 pounds European cucumbers or regular cucumbers

¼ cup salt

1 quart buttermilk

⅔ cup chopped fresh dill + dill for garnish

3 tablespoons unsalted butter, whole

½ cup shallots, minced fine

½ pound fresh shrimp, peeled and cut into ½-inch pieces

1 cup dry vermouth

dill vinegar or red wine vinegar

salt and freshly ground black pepper

½ cup razor red onions (see note)

½ cup fresh tomato concassé (page 237)

PREPARATION

1. Peel the cucumbers. Using a small spoon, or a melon baller, scrape the seeds out. Cut into ½-inch pieces; toss the cucumbers with the salt and transfer to a colander set over a bowl. Refrigerate for 2 to 3 hours or overnight.

2. Transfer the cucumbers to a blender or food processor, discarding all exuded juices. Purée until smooth; pass through a food mill if desired. Whisk in the buttermilk and dill; set aside.

3. Melt the butter in a sauté pan over medium heat. When the butter foams, add the shallots and cook 30 seconds. Add the shrimp and stir over medium heat 10 to 15 seconds. Add the vermouth, bring to a boil, and immediately strain into the reserved cucumber soup. Spread the shrimp and shallot mixture on a plate to cool, then refrigerate. Chill the soup.

4. To serve: adjust the consistency of the soup with more buttermilk if necessary. Season with vinegar, salt (add sparingly; it probably won't need much), and pepper to taste. Divide the shrimp between chilled soup plates. Ladle the soup over the shrimp and garnish with red onion, tomato concassé, and bits of dill strewn about.

Note: Razor red onions are red onions sliced paper-thin and then tossed with a pinch of sugar and enough lemon juice to coat them. Prepare 1 to 2 hours ahead and toss occasionally, until softened and pink.

Cream of Vidalia Onion Soup

SERVES 8

We have been making this soup since our days at the Fearrington House. In fact, the original appeared in the late Jenny Fitch's compilation of recipes from that restaurant. Cool, elegant, and very refined, it is obviously Southern vichyssoise without the potatoes—perfect for a late spring lunch al fresco.

INGREDIENTS

4 ounces smoked country bacon, julienned

½ cup (1 stick) unsalted butter

3 pounds Vidalia onions, thinly sliced (or substitute Maui or Walla Walla onions)

8 cloves garlic, peeled and left whole

2 cups dry white wine

1 quart chicken stock, preferably homemade

1 bay leaf

1 tablespoon fresh thyme

1 cup crème fraîche, heavy cream, or sour cream

salt, freshly ground white pepper, Tabasco, and nutmeg to taste

zest of 2 lemons, grated (or to taste)

dash lemon juice (to taste)

2 cups homemade herb croutons (page 243)

3 tablespoons chives, snipped

1½ tablespoons chive petals, plucked from blossoms (optional)

PREPARATION

1. Cook the bacon slowly until crisp. Remove to paper toweling and reserve. Add the butter, onions, and garlic to the bacon renderings, cover, and cook over low heat, stirring often, until the onions are translucent and lightly caramelized. Add the wine, stock, bay leaf, and thyme; bring to a boil and simmer 30 minutes.

2. Remove the bay leaf and purée the soup in a food processor or blender, in batches if necessary. Pass the soup through the fine blade of a food mill (optional). Chill.

3. Whisk in the cream, crème fraîche, or sour cream. Season with salt, white pepper, Tabasco, and nutmeg. Add lemon zest and juice to taste. Serve in chilled bowls. Garnish with the reserved bacon, croutons, chives, and optional chive blossoms.

Note: This soup may also be served hot; if you choose to do this, use cream or crème fraîche, not sour cream, so the soup won't curdle.

Curried Butternut Soup with Shrimp & Toasted Coconut

SERVES 8

The texture of cooked butternuts is incomparable in soup. Roasting them before cooking in the broth adds depth and accentuates their sweetness. It is worth it to make your own curry spice in small batches and keep it refrigerated in a jar. It will lend added complexity to this autumn mainstay.

INGREDIENTS FOR THE SOUP

- 2 pounds butternut squash, peeled, seeded, and cut into 1-inch chunks
- ½ cup clarified butter (page 243)
- 1 onion, peeled and sliced
- 2 carrots, peeled and sliced
- ½ cup chopped garlic
- ½ cup peeled, chopped fresh ginger
- 2 jalapeños or 3–4 serranos, sliced, with seeds
- ¼ cup curry spice (page 244) or Madras curry blend
- 1 large tart apple (e.g., Granny Smith), peeled, cored, and cut into dice
- 1 quart homemade chicken stock
- 1 can unsweetened coconut milk
- salt, freshly ground black pepper, and cider vinegar to taste
- 1 orange

INGREDIENTS FOR THE GARNISH

- 2 tablespoons mango chutney (we use Major Grey's), chopped fine
- ⅓ cup heavy cream, lightly whipped
- ½ cup combined chopped fresh mint and cilantro leaves
- ¼ cup dried currants, plumped in ¼ cup hot water and then drained
- ½ pound medium shrimp, peeled and split lengthwise, or bay scallops, muscle removed; cooked in a little butter
- ½ cup unsweetened coconut, lightly toasted

PREPARATION

1. Preheat oven to 400°. Toss the squash in 2 tablespoons clarified butter and bake, covered, for 30 minutes.
2. In a 4-quart heavy-bottomed pan, heat 6 tablespoons clarified butter over medium heat. Add the onions and carrots, cover, and cook 15 minutes, stirring occasionally, until the vegetables are softened.
3. Add the garlic, ginger, jalapeños or serranos, and curry; cook 1 minute, then stir in the roasted squash and the apple chunks. Add the stock, bring to a boil, and reduce to a simmer. Cook, uncovered, for 20 to 30 minutes, or until the vegetables are very tender.

4. Cool the soup slightly and then purée in a blender or processor in batches. Pass through a food mill. Whisk in the coconut milk. The soup may be prepared ahead to this point.

5. Rewarm the soup over low heat, stirring. Adjust the consistency with more chicken stock if desired. Season generously with salt, pepper, and cider vinegar. Grate the zest of the orange into the soup. Keep warm.

6. For garnish, fold the mango chutney into the whipped cream and reserve. Divide the herbs, currants, and shrimp between warm bowls. Ladle hot soup into each. Spoon a dollop of mango chantilly in the center of each and sprinkle with coconut. Serve immediately.

New Orleans Red Bean Soup with Andouille & Rice

SERVES 8

We went to New Orleans for a belated honeymoon in 1982, and one day we had lunch at a dive, Mena's Palace, on the periphery of the French Quarter. We experienced a red beans and rice epiphany, and those flavors were filed away, to be recreated in this soup. Like all bean soups, this one benefits from being made a day or so ahead, to allow the flavors to meld.

INGREDIENTS FOR THE SOUP

    1 pound small red beans, picked over

    4 ounces andouille sausage

    ½ cup olive oil

    1 smoked ham hock

    1 cup onion, cut into small dice

    ½ cup green bell pepper, cut into small dice

    ½ cup red bell pepper, cut into small dice

    2 ribs celery, cut into small dice

    1 poblano chile, cut into small dice (optional)

    1 jalapeño, chopped, with seeds

    ½ cup chopped garlic

    1 bay leaf

    2 tablespoons Creole spice blend (page 243)

    1 cup seeded, canned tomatoes, chopped, with juice reserved

    ½ cup strained juice from tomatoes

    1 ½ quarts light chicken stock

    salt, black pepper, Tabasco, and cider vinegar to taste

INGREDIENTS FOR THE GARNISH

    1 cup cooked long-grain white rice

    ¼ pound smoked turkey in 1 slice, cut into ½-inch cubes

    2 tablespoons each chopped parsley, oregano, and basil

    tomato concassé (page 237)

    1 cup scallions, trimmed and sliced on the bias

1. The night before, pick through the red beans to remove any debris, small stones, and split beans. Rinse the beans, transfer to a container, cover with double their volume of cold water, and refrigerate overnight. Drain the next day and proceed with the recipe.

2. Cut the andouille sausage in half lengthwise, then crosswise into ½-inch pieces. Heat the olive oil over medium heat, add the sausage, and cook until lightly browned. Remove the sausage and drain on a paper towel.

3. In the reserved oil, brown the ham hock on all sides for 5 minutes. Add the onion, red and green peppers, and celery and cook over medium heat until the vegetables are softened and begin to caramelize on the edges. Add the poblano, jalapeño, garlic, bay leaf, and Creole spice. Cook 2 minutes, stirring. Add the tomatoes, ½ cup of their juice, and the red beans and bring to a simmer. Add the chicken stock; bring to a boil and cook at a simmer until the beans are done. Remove the hock; cut the meat off, mince it, and return it to the soup. Remove the bay leaf.

4. Add salt to taste, then remove 1 cup of beans and vegetables and purée in a food processor. Stir the purée into the soup. (The soup is best made ahead to this point.) Warm the soup over low heat and adjust the consistency with more stock or water if necessary. Season with more salt if necessary and with pepper, Tabasco, and cider vinegar to taste. Keep hot.

TO SERVE

Into each of 8 large, warm bowls, spoon 2 tablespoons of cooked rice. Divide the sausage, herbs, and smoked turkey between the bowls. Stir the soup and divide it between the bowls. Garnish with tomato concassé. Sprinkle with scallions. Serve immediately, with more Tabasco on the side for those who desire it.

Moroccan Roasted Eggplant Bisque with Grilled Chicken & Minted Yogurt

SERVES 10 TO 12

This is one of the all-time favorites of the service staff at the Grill. The complex layers of flavors in the soup are balanced by the sumptuous texture of the eggplant and the smokiness of the chicken. You can lower the heat level by leaving out the seeds from the jalapeños, or eliminating the chiles entirely, or you can explore the opposite end of the spectrum and excite your heat-loving pals by upping the amount of chiles.

INGREDIENTS FOR THE BISQUE

2 large eggplants (about 2 pounds)
½ cup olive oil
2 large onions, sliced (1½ cups)
2 jalapeños, stemmed and chopped, with seeds
8 cloves garlic, peeled and left whole
2 tablespoons Moroccan spice blend (page 244)

generous pinch saffron

1 cinnamon stick

1 bay leaf

2 cups canned tomatoes, seeded and chopped, with juices strained and reserved

1 ½ quarts chicken stock

salt and black pepper to taste

zest of 1 lemon, grated

¼ cup lemon juice, or more to taste

¼ cup chopped cilantro

¼ cup slivered fresh mint

PREPARATION

1. Preheat oven to 350°. Prick the eggplants in several places with a fork and roast on a baking sheet for 30 to 40 minutes, until soft and partially collapsed. Remove from the oven, split, and cool on the baking sheet. When cool enough to handle, remove the skin and discard. Scrape the seeds if the eggplants are excessively seedy. Reserve the roasted flesh.

2. Heat the olive oil over medium heat. Add the onions and cook until softened. Add the garlic cloves, jalapeños, Moroccan spice, saffron, bay leaf, and cinnamon stick. Cook 2 minutes and then add the tomatoes, with their juices, and the roasted eggplant. Stir in the chicken stock, bring to a simmer, and cook 20 to 30 minutes. Remove the cinnamon stick and bay leaf and purée the soup in batches in a food processor. Pass through a food mill if desired. Cool and reserve, refrigerated.

INGREDIENTS FOR THE GARNISH AND ASSEMBLY

½ pound boneless, skinless chicken thighs

1 tablespoon Moroccan spice blend (page 244)

olive oil

6 ounces plain yogurt

1 tablespoon slivered fresh mint

½ cup pitted, slivered calamata olives

⅓ cup cilantro leaves

PREPARATION FOR THE GARNISH

1. Rub the chicken thighs with the spice blend and enough olive oil to coat. Season with salt and grill until charred and just cooked through, about 10 minutes. (You may also bake the thighs on a rack for 15 minutes in a 350° oven.) Cool slightly and cut into ½-inch chunks. Reserve.

2. Combine the yogurt with the slivered mint and set aside, refrigerated.

ASSEMBLY

Rewarm the soup over medium-low heat, stirring often. Adjust the consistency with stock if necessary. Season with salt, pepper, lemon zest, and lemon juice to taste. Divide the chicken, cilantro, and mint between bowls. Ladle hot soup into the bowls, spoon a dollop of yogurt into the center, and sprinkle with slivered olives and cilantro leaves. Serve immediately.

Summersweet Corn Bisque with Shiitake Mushrooms, Bacon, & Truffle Oil

SERVES 10

Like many Southerners, we grew up believing Silver Queen is the ultimate variety of corn. Now there are numerous hybrid "supersweet" corn types that delay the natural conversion of sugars to starch, but they often taste unnaturally sweet. Ideally, use just-picked white corn (or yellow, if that's your preference).

If you have fresh chanterelles available, by all means use them in place of the shiitake mushrooms.

8 cups Summersweet or Silver Queen corn, kernels cut from cob,
   with cob scraped and reserved

7 cups chicken stock, to yield 6 cups corn stock (see step 1 below)

½ pound small shiitake mushrooms with stems removed and reserved and
   caps sliced ¼ inch thick

4 ounces sliced bacon, cut crosswise into ½-inch strips

4 leeks, trimmed, halved, sliced crosswise ½-inch thick, washed, and drained

6 cloves garlic, peeled and minced

2 bay leaves

1 cup dry sherry

1 cup white wine

1 cup crème fraîche or heavy cream

salt, black pepper, nutmeg, and sherry vinegar to taste

1 tablespoon whole unsalted butter

2 tablespoons olive oil

2 tablespoons fresh thyme leaves

2 tablespoons fresh marjoram leaves

¼ cup snipped chives

truffle oil (optional)

PREPARATION

1. Cut the corn off the cob with a knife. Using the back of the knife, scrape the
   milk off the cobs. Reserve the corn and make corn stock by placing the cobs in
   a large pot with 7 cups chicken stock. Bring to a boil, add the shiitake stems,
   reduce to a simmer, and cook 15 minutes. Strain and set aside.

2. Cook the bacon until crisp; remove and drain on a paper towel. In the rendered
   bacon fat, cook the drained leeks over medium heat until soft. Add the garlic,
   bay leaves, and corn; cook 3 minutes. Add the sherry and wine and bring to a
   boil, stirring.

3. Add the strained corn stock, bring to a simmer, and cook 15 minutes,
   until the vegetables are tender. Remove the bay leaves. Purée the soup with
   a hand immersion mixer *or* purée half of it in a blender and combine with
   the remainder. Whisk in the crème fraîche (or cream). Warm over low heat;
   season with salt, pepper, and nutmeg and adjust the acidity with sherry vinegar.
   Keep warm.

4. Sauté the sliced shiitake mushroom caps in the whole butter and olive oil over
   medium-high heat, stirring often. Season with salt, pepper, and a dash or two
   of sherry vinegar. Stir in the thyme and marjoram.

5. Divide the shiitakes into warm bowls.

6. Stir the bisque and ladle into bowls. Sprinkle with crisp bacon and chives;
   drizzle a little truffle oil on each and serve immediately.

appetizers

Grilled Fresh Figs with Prosciutto
(or Country Ham) & Maytag Blue Mousse

Marinated Goat Cheese on Warm Field Peas
Vinaigrette

Grilled Asparagus Salad with Wild & Exotic
Mushrooms, Country Bacon, & Truffled Eggs

Wild & Exotic Mushroom Salad on
Marinated Nebraska Wedding Tomatoes
with Warm Sherry-Bacon Vinaigrette

Romaine Salad with Texas Ruby Red Grapefruit
& Roquefort in Pomegranate-Port Vinaigrette

Softshell Crabs in Cornmeal Tempura with
Fennel Slaw & Tomato Aioli

Spicy Grilled Shrimp with Grits Cake,
Country Ham, & Redeye Vinaigrette

Shrimp Chiles Rellenos with Chipotle-Tomato
Vinaigrette & Avocado Salsa

Pork & Crawfish Potsticker Dumplings
with Spicy Cajun Cream

Pickled Shrimp with Crab & Pepper Slaw
& Smoked Tomato Remoulade

Hot Smoked (or Grilled) Oysters with
Preserved Lemon & Caviar

Fried Oysters on Creamy Winter Succotash
with Barbecue Vinaigrette

Crab Cakes with Sauce Diable
& Corn Relish Salad

Black Bass Sashimi with Warm Thai "Shrimp"
Vinaigrette

Crisp Peppered Quail with Country Ham
& Spicy Crawfish Hominy

Roast Saddle of Rabbit Wrapped in
Country Ham on Warm Brunswick Stew
& Wild Watercress Salad

Grilled Fresh Figs with Prosciutto (or Country Ham) & Maytag Blue Mousse

SERVES 8

While not an uncommon treatment for fresh figs, this preparation demonstrates the extraordinary juxtaposition of several simple, perfect ingredients. When figs are in season, this dish is often on our menu; we never cease to be amazed at the positive response it generates. People swoon over these figs.

Whether you have a fig tree of your own or you are purchasing your figs, look for ones that are firm but ripe, with minute separation in the skin near the blossom end. Often you will be competing with the birds, who seem to know the exact moment when figs reach perfect ripeness.

If you wish, the figs may be roasted in a hot oven or glazed under the broiler in lieu of firing up the grill.

INGREDIENTS

16 fresh figs, Mission or Brown Turkey, washed
4 ounces Maytag blue cheese, at room temperature
   (Roquefort or Gorgonzola dolce also work well)
4 ounces mascarpone, at room temperature
freshly ground black pepper
¾ cup balsamic vinegar
⅓ cup basil vinaigrette (see recipe below) or another vinaigrette if you prefer
6 ounces prosciutto, sliced paper-thin
½ pound baby lettuces, or mesclun mix, washed and dried
½ cup basil oil (page 240), made 1 day in advance, if using, or extra virgin olive oil

PREPARATION

1. Cream the Maytag and mascarpone together in a small bowl. Season with black pepper and set aside, covered.
2. In a small nonreactive saucepan, cook the balsamic vinegar over medium heat until reduced to 3 or 4 tablespoons and syrupy. Cool and reserve at room temperature. Make the basil vinaigrette (see below).
3. Starting at the stem end, split the figs three-quarters of the way down, leaving the bottom intact. Stuff each fig with 1 to 1½ tablespoons of the cheese mixture. Cut the prosciutto slices lengthwise. Wrap a strip of prosciutto around each fig, being sure to cover the bottom and as much of the stuffed section as possible. Refrigerate if not preparing immediately, but remove from refrigeration 15 minutes before cooking.
4. Light a charcoal grill and let the fire cook down to medium-hot. Grill the figs, bottom-side down, until the prosciutto is crisp and the figs are warm.
5. Toss the lettuces in the basil vinaigrette (or one of your choosing) and divide between 8 room-temperature plates. Place 2 figs on each plate. Combine the balsamic syrup and basil (or olive) oil; stir and drizzle over the figs and around each plate. Grind fresh black pepper over all and serve immediately.

BASIL VINAIGRETTE
    2 tablespoons balsamic vinegar
    ¼ cup basil oil (page 240)
    salt and black pepper to taste

Whisk together. Season and reserve.

Marinated Goat Cheese on
Warm Field Peas Vinaigrette

SERVES 8

We have been fortunate to have Fleming Pfann's Celebrity Dairy goat cheese on our menu almost year-round. When you're working with an artisanal product like cheese, you have to adapt to seasonal variations in the milk, when the goats are nursing or their diet changes. This recipe is wonderful with summer cheese, slightly leaner and more tangy, and the first shelled purple hull peas, delicate and earthy.

You can use any fresh goat cheese in log form; Laurel Chenel's from California or Coach Farm from New York is exceptional. You can use frozen peas, but dried peas lack the delicacy this dish demands.

INGREDIENTS FOR THE GOAT CHEESE
>   1 log fresh goat cheese (about 12 ounces)
>   3 cloves garlic, mashed
>   zest of 1 lemon, coarsely chopped
>   4–5 sprigs fresh lemon thyme
>   3–4 sprigs fresh marjoram
>   freshly ground black pepper
>   ¾ cup fruity, extra virgin olive oil

PREPARATION
>   1. Cut the goat cheese into 8 discs. We use dental floss or sewing thread to make clean cuts through the soft, fresh cheese.
>   2. Combine the remaining ingredients in a glass dish. Roll each disc in this marinade and set aside, covered, for 4 hours or longer. If refrigerated, let sit at room temperature for at least 2 hours before serving.

2 ounces olive oil

½ cup sweet onion, finely diced

¼ cup carrot, peeled and finely diced

2 tablespoons minced garlic

1 bay leaf

pinch crushed red pepper flakes

2 pints fresh, shelled purple hull (or other) peas

2 cups vegetable stock or light chicken stock

salt and black pepper to taste

¼ cup mint vinegar (page 242)

¼ cup extra virgin olive oil

2 tablespoons mint leaves, cut into chiffonade, divided
    (reserve 1 tablespoon for garnish)

1 tablespoon lemon thyme leaves

1 tablespoon marjoram leaves

1 roasted red bell pepper, peeled and cut into julienne

PREPARATION

1. Heat the olive oil over medium heat. Add the onion and carrots, reduce to
   low heat, and cook, covered, until the vegetables are soft. Stir in the garlic,
   bay leaf, and red pepper flakes and cook 2 minutes. Add the peas and stock,
   bring to a gentle simmer, and cook until the peas are tender but still retain their
   fresh texture. Most of the stock will be absorbed. Season with salt and pepper.
   Cool quickly and refrigerate if not using immediately.
2. To serve: combine the mint vinegar and extra virgin olive oil and set aside.
   Warm the peas over medium heat until heated through; check the seasoning.
   Add the vinaigrette and herbs, stirring to combine. Divide the peas onto
   8 plates. Place a marinated disc of cheese on the peas and scatter some roasted
   pepper and mint leaf chiffonade over all.

Grilled Asparagus Salad with Wild & Exotic Mushrooms, Country Bacon, & Truffled Eggs

SERVES 8

This is one of our favorite spring salads: smoky, nutty asparagus, earthy mushrooms, the poached egg yolk oozing into the salad, and the heady aroma of truffle combine to meld many wonderful flavors into one dish. The first large asparagus of spring are often tender enough not to peel, but, aesthetically, they look more refined prepared that way. If you choose to use the black truffle instead of the truffle oil, store it with the eggs for the dish in a closed container for 1 to 2 days, so the eggs absorb the truffle aroma.

This is an example of how we take a great flavor profile and apply it to the ingredients of the season. For another example, see the recipe that follows.

INGREDIENTS FOR THE ASPARAGUS SALAD

32 large asparagus spears, snapped, peeled if necessary, blanched crisp-tender, cooled in ice water, and drained

16 wooden skewers, soaked in cold water for 1 hour

zest of 1 lemon, grated

¼ cup olive oil

freshly ground black pepper

salt

3 cups spicy field greens, such as mizzuna, arugula, watercress, and frisée, cleaned

8 poached eggs (see page 30 for poaching procedure)

herb croutons (page 243)

2 teaspoons each fresh thyme leaves, chervil, and parsley, combined

1 ½ ounces fresh black summer truffle, brushed, sliced, and julienned (or use white truffle oil)

1 tablespoon chives, snipped ¼ inch long

INGREDIENTS FOR THE VINAIGRETTE

1 pound mixed wild and/or exotic mushrooms, such as morels, chanterelles, hedgehogs, black trumpets, shiitake, or cremini, trimmed, cleaned, and cut into halves or quarters

4 ounces olive oil + oil for cooking mushrooms

4 ounces country smoked slab bacon, cut into lardons (large julienne)

½ cup sherry vinegar

2 tablespoons wildflower honey

1 tablespoon garlic, minced

2 tablespoons shallots, minced

salt and black pepper

PREPARATION

1. Place 4 asparagus flat on a work surface. Insert a skewer perpendicularly through all 4 asparagus near the tip end. Insert a second skewer parallel near the stem end. Repeat with the remaining asparagus. Gently coat the skewered asparagus with the lemon zest, olive oil, pepper, and salt and set aside.

2. Make mushroom vinaigrette. Sauté the mushrooms in batches in olive oil, season, and transfer to paper toweling to drain. In the same pan, cook the bacon until rendered but still tender. Remove to drain. In a bowl, combine the vinegar and honey. Add 4 ounces olive oil to the pan with the bacon renderings and heat until shimmering; add the garlic and shallots and pour over the vinegar-honey mixture. Whisk to combine; season and reserve.

3. Light the grill and cook down to a medium fire. Meanwhile, warm the mushrooms over low heat, put the cleaned greens in a large bowl, and poach the eggs (or rewarm over low heat if cooked in advance). Grill the asparagus until warm and lightly charred. Arrange 4 asparagus in a fan on each plate. Raise the heat under the mushrooms, add the vinaigrette, and heat until simmering. Pour over the greens and toss with the croutons, bacon, and herbs.

Divide between the plates, placing the greens at the base of the asparagus spears.

4. Top each salad with a poached egg; season the egg and drizzle with the remaining vinaigrette. Sprinkle with the truffle, or truffle oil, and chives. Serve immediately.

Wild & Exotic Mushroom Salad on Marinated Nebraska Wedding Tomatoes with Warm Sherry-Bacon Vinaigrette

SERVES 8

Well, bacon and tomatoes. And mushrooms. The synergy of this dish, with its woodsy aromatics, smoky bacon, and herbal punch against prime summer tomatoes, makes for a resounding first course—warm against cool, tangy against sweet. And if you grow your own tomatoes and forage for wild mushrooms, the experience is almost free. The tomato fondue isn't essential to the dish but adds a concentrated tomato acidity to the overall flavor.

INGREDIENTS FOR THE ROASTED TOMATO FONDUE (OPTIONAL)

1 pound very ripe roma tomatoes

3 tablespoons olive oil

2 tablespoons sherry vinegar

2 tablespoons fino sherry

INGREDIENTS FOR THE TOMATOES

2 pounds yellow heirloom tomatoes (e.g., Nebraska Wedding, yellow Giant Belgium, yellow Brandywine) or low- to medium-acid tomatoes, yellow or red

2 shallots, minced

1 teaspoon tarragon, minced

extra virgin olive oil

freshly ground black pepper

salt

INGREDIENTS FOR THE MUSHROOM SALAD

1½ pounds mixed wild/exotic mushrooms, at least 3 different varieties (chanterelles, hedgehogs, black trumpets, shiitakes, oysters, cremini)

olive oil for sautéing

salt and black pepper

4 cups combined watercress and frisée (you may blend in endive, arugula, or other sturdy, pungent lettuces)

1 cup sweet onion, peeled and shaved paper-thin (we use a Japanese mandoline)

¼ cup combined tarragon and parsley, chopped

INGREDIENTS FOR THE VINAIGRETTE

 4 ounces country-sliced smoked bacon, cut crosswise into julienne

 3 ounces extra virgin olive oil

 1 teaspoon garlic, minced

 1 tablespoon shallot, minced

 ¼ cup sherry vinegar

 2 tablespoons fino sherry

 salt and black pepper

INGREDIENTS FOR THE GARNISH

 2 tablespoons extra virgin olive oil

 reserved crisp bacon, chopped

 1 tablespoon tarragon leaves, cut into fine chiffonade

PREPARATION

1. Make the roasted tomato fondue. Preheat oven to 350°. Cut the tomatoes in half, toss with the olive oil, and roast on a sheet pan for 35 to 40 minutes, until softened and lightly browned. Purée through a food mill and then combine the purée with the sherry and vinegar in a nonreactive saucepot. Bring to a boil, reduce the heat to medium, and cook, stirring frequently, until thickened to the consistency of hot fudge. Season with salt and adjust the acidity; reserve at room temperature.

2. Marinate the tomatoes. Slice the tomatoes as thinly as possible. Combine the shallots, tarragon, olive oil, black pepper and salt and drizzle the mixture over the tomatoes. Cover and reserve at room temperature for 1 to 2 hours.

3. Clean, trim, and cut the mushrooms into wedges (or slice if you prefer), discarding the trimmings. Heat a heavy-bottomed sauté pan over medium-high heat. Add olive oil and sauté the mushrooms, seasoned with salt and pepper, until browned. (Sauté the mushrooms in batches if necessary.) Drain on paper toweling and reserve.

4. Clean the greens, dry, tear into small pieces, and reserve.

5. Make the vinaigrette. In a heavy-bottomed steel or cast-iron pan, cook the bacon over medium heat until crisp. Remove the cooked bacon, reserving it at room temperature, and leave the rendered fat in the pan. Heat the rendered bacon fat with 3 ounces of olive oil over medium-high heat until aromatic but not smoking. Add the minced garlic and shallot and cook for 15 seconds, without scorching. Pour the hot oil into a heavy bowl and immediately add the vinegar, sherry, and salt and pepper to taste. Adjust the acidity; the vinaigrette should be tart.

6. To serve: arrange the marinated tomatoes on 6 plates. Season with salt. Place the greens, shaved onion, and chopped parsley and tarragon in a large stainless bowl. Heat a large sauté pan over medium-high heat, film with olive oil, and sauté the mushrooms to warm through. Stir the vinaigrette *well*, add to the mushrooms, and pour over the greens. Toss to wilt lightly, season, and divide between the plates. Drizzle tomato fondue and extra virgin olive oil around the outside. Sprinkle with reserved crisp bacon and tarragon chiffonade.

Romaine Salad with Texas Ruby Red Grapefruit & Roquefort in Pomegranate-Port Vinaigrette

SERVES 8

This somewhat incongruous combination of ingredients yields one of our favorite salads: visually, the deep pink grapefruit, blue-veined cheese, and "jewels" of pomegranate seeds on crisp lettuces are dramatic. The flavors integrate sweet, salty, and tangy, and come with a textural crunch. Serve this salad in December and January, when you desire a light but complex salad to precede a roast or braised dish.

INGREDIENTS

    8 cups romaine hearts, cleaned and torn
    pomegranate-port vinaigrette (see recipe below)
    salt and black pepper to taste
    2½ cups ruby red grapefruit segments (about 2 grapefruit)
    ¾ cup Roquefort, crumbled
    ¾ cup walnuts, lightly toasted and skins rubbed off
    seeds from 1 ripe pomegranate (see note)

PREPARATION

    Dress the romaine with the pomegranate-port vinaigrette and season with salt and pepper. Divide between 8 chilled plates. Divide the grapefruit segments between the salads. Sprinkle crumbled Roquefort, then walnuts, and finally pomegranate seeds on top of the salads. Serve immediately.

Note: Fresh pomegranates usually are available from November until January. Look for deep red fruit with firm skins and heavy weight for their size. Cut the fruit in half, pick the seeds from the membrane, and keep refrigerated until ready to use.

INGREDIENTS FOR THE POMEGRANATE-PORT VINAIGRETTE

    ⅓ cup ruby port
    ⅓ cup orange juice
    1 cup pomegranate juice (or cranberry juice)
    1 teaspoon minced garlic
    1 tablespoon shallots, minced
    1 egg yolk
    2 tablespoons red wine vinegar
    ½ cup safflower or peanut oil
    2 tablespoons walnut oil
    salt and black pepper to taste

PREPARATION

    1. Combine the port, juices, and garlic in a nonreactive saucepot. Bring to a boil and simmer until reduced to ⅓ cup. Put the shallots in a stainless bowl, strain the reduction over them, and cool.

2. Add the egg yolk, reduction, and red wine vinegar to a bowl and whisk to combine. Combine the safflower and walnut oils and drizzle into the yolk mixture, whisking to emulsify. Season with salt and pepper and reserve. Refrigerate if not using immediately.

Softshell Crabs in Cornmeal Tempura with Fennel Slaw & Tomato Aioli

SERVES 4 AS AN APPETIZER OR 2 AS AN ENTRÉE

One of our deathbed requests will be for softshell crabs; with luck, they'll be in season. In late spring and early summer, molting Atlantic blue crabs are one of life's finest pleasures. Shigeru Matsuyama, a fine Japanese chef who cooked with us for several years, taught us this tempura recipe; we made it Southern with the addition of cornmeal—which has the added benefit of keeping the crabs crisper longer.

The fennel slaw and tomato aioli add textural contrast, acidic foil, and visual appeal, while still allowing the "star" of the plate to shine through.

INGREDIENTS FOR THE CRABS

4 jumbo softshell crabs, cleaned (see note)
1 egg yolk
1 cup ice cubes + 1 cup water (to yield 2 cups)
½ teaspoon baking powder
1 cup flour, sifted
1 cup stone-ground yellow cornmeal
⅛ teaspoon cayenne pepper
¼ teaspoon salt
2 tablespoons fresh basil, minced
peanut oil for frying

INGREDIENTS FOR THE SLAW

2 tablespoons tarragon vinegar
2 tablespoons lemon juice
1 teaspoon sugar
pinch crushed red pepper flakes
1 cup fennel bulb, trimmed, with tops reserved, cored, and shaved paper-thin with a Japanese mandoline, or by hand
⅓ cup red onion, shaved paper-thin
1 carrot, peeled and cut into fine julienne
½ cup red bell pepper, cut into fine julienne
¼ cup basil leaves, torn into pieces
¼ cup Italian parsley leaves
2 tablespoons chopped fennel tops
salt and black pepper to taste
¼ cup scallions, sliced crosswise, for garnish

2 tablespoons tarragon vinegar

2 tablespoons roasted garlic purée (page 245)

1 egg yolk, at room temperature

1 teaspoon tomato paste

½ cup olive oil

⅓ cup tomato concassé (page 237)

Tabasco, salt, and black pepper to taste

PREPARATION

1. Make the tempura batter for the crabs. Beat the egg yolk in a bowl; stir in the ice water. Combine the baking powder, flour, cornmeal, and cayenne and whisk into the egg mixture. Season with salt and stir in the basil. Refrigerate for 1 hour or longer.

2. Make the slaw. Combine the vinegar and lemon juice with the sugar and red pepper flakes. Pour over the fennel, onion, carrot, and pepper and toss to mix; season and refrigerate for 1 hour. Toss with the basil, parsley, and fennel tops just before serving.

3. Make the aioli. In a bowl, combine the vinegar, roasted garlic purée, egg yolk, and tomato paste; whisk in the olive oil in a steady stream to emulsify. Fold in the tomato concassé and season with salt, pepper, and Tabasco. Reserve.

4. Heat peanut oil in a deep fryer or heavy-bottomed pot to 350° (use a deep-frying thermometer). Stir the tempura batter well. Immerse the crabs in the tempura batter to coat thoroughly and then drain on a rack for a few seconds. Carefully slip the crabs into the hot oil, one at a time. Be cautious, as they may splatter. Fry for 1 minute, turning with tongs if necessary. Carefully remove to rack and keep hot.

5. Divide the slaw between 4 plates. Place a hot crab to the side of the slaw and spoon aioli onto the plate and over the crab. Sprinkle with scallions and serve immediately.

Note: To clean crabs, lift the shell flaps on each side and cut out the "breathers," the fingerlike gills, which can be bitter. Cut the crab's face off just behind the eyes. Turn over and lift the "apron" flap on the bottom and cut off. Or, if all of this is just too gross, have your fishmonger clean them for you. Buy your softshells on the day you plan to cook them; they should be alive. Avoid dead crabs, as they deteriorate rapidly once they expire; we personally can't recommend frozen softshells, but some people find them acceptable.

Spicy Grilled Shrimp with Grits Cake, Country Ham, & Redeye Vinaigrette

SERVES 8 AS A FIRST COURSE

What can we say about shrimp and grits? The late Bill Neal popularized this traditional low country breakfast dish at his own Crook's Corner in Chapel Hill. We love the flavor combination of country ham, grits, and "redeye gravy," so this rendition combines shrimp and our uptown version of "redeye" as both a vinaigrette and a sauce for grilled shrimp and a rich grits cake.

All the components can be made well in advance, then finished and assembled at the last moment.

INGREDIENTS FOR THE GRITS CAKES

    1 quart chicken stock
    1 teaspoon salt
    1 cup fine white or yellow grits (not instant or quick-cooking)
    2 large eggs
    4 egg yolks
    1 cup Parmesan or Sonoma Dry Jack cheese, grated
    salt, freshly ground black pepper, and Tabasco to taste
    2 tablespoons unsalted butter for greasing the baking pan

PREPARATION

    1. Preheat oven to 350°. Generously butter an 8 × 11-inch baking pan (or
       jelly roll pan). Over high heat, bring the chicken stock to a boil in a 3-quart
       saucepot. Stir in the salt and grits, reduce the heat to medium, and cook,
       stirring frequently, until the grits have thickened and are just beginning to
       pull away from the sides of the pan.

    2. Whisk the eggs and yolks in a bowl. Temper the eggs by whisking a spoonful
       of hot grits into the bowl (this prevents the eggs from scrambling in the grits).
       Whisk the eggs into the grits until well combined. Stir in the cheese and season
       well with salt, black pepper, and Tabasco. Spread evenly into the buttered pan
       and bake 25 to 30 minutes until the mixture is set: it will be firm and have a
       lightly mottled surface. Cool on a rack. Refrigerate to firm up.

    3. Using a biscuit cutter, cut 8 2½- to 3-inch rounds in the grits and transfer
       to a lightly greased baking sheet. Reserve. (Save the grits scraps—heated
       and topped with sautéed mushrooms, they make a satisfying rustic snack
       or lunch.)

INGREDIENTS FOR THE SHRIMP

    1½ pounds (15–20 count) large shrimp, peeled to last tail section,
       with shells reserved
    16 6-inch wooden skewers, soaked in cold water for 30 minutes
    1 teaspoon cracked fennel seed
    zest of 1 lemon, grated

1 teaspoon crushed red pepper flakes

6 cloves garlic, peeled and mashed

1 teaspoon freshly ground black pepper

⅓ cup cold-pressed peanut oil (or olive oil)

PREPARATION

1. Divide the shrimp into 8 equal portions. Line up a portion on a work surface and insert one skewer through the head section of the shrimp and a second skewer through the tail section, parallel to the first. This facilitates turning the shrimp, keeps them from curling, and promotes even cooking. Repeat with the remaining portions.

2. Combine the fennel seed, lemon zest, red pepper flakes, garlic, black pepper, and oil. Marinate the shrimp skewers in this mixture, refrigerated, for 2 to 4 hours, turning occasionally.

INGREDIENTS FOR THE SHRIMP OIL

1 cup cold-pressed peanut oil (or olive oil)

reserved shrimp shells

1 teaspoon tomato paste

PREPARATION

Heat 2 tablespoons of the peanut oil until shimmering. Stir in the reserved shrimp shells and cook 2 minutes. Stir in the tomato paste, add the remaining oil, and heat to a bare simmer. Remove from heat and steep 2 hours or longer. Strain through cheesecloth or a fine strainer, pressing on the shells. Reserve at room temperature.

INGREDIENTS FOR THE VINAIGRETTE

2 tablespoons peanut oil

4 ounces thinly sliced country ham, trimmed of all fat and julienned

3 tablespoons strong black coffee

½ cup balsamic vinegar

1 cup chicken stock

1 tablespoon garlic, peeled and finely minced

½ teaspoon crushed red pepper flakes

shrimp oil (see above)

2 tablespoons fresh thyme leaves

PREPARATION

1. Heat the peanut oil in an 8-inch cast-iron skillet or sauté pan over medium-high heat. Cook the julienned country ham until lightly browned. Remove to a paper towel to drain and pour off the fat from the pan.

2. Deglaze the pan with black coffee. Add the balsamic vinegar, bring to a boil, and reduce by half. Add the chicken stock, bring to a simmer, and reduce by two-thirds. Stir in the garlic and red pepper flakes. Cool, strain, and then whisk in the shrimp oil and fresh thyme. Set aside.

salt to taste

½ pound mesclun, or mixed young, peppery greens, washed and dried

fresh thyme leaves for garnish

ASSEMBLY

1. Light the grill and let the coals burn down to a medium-hot fire. Preheat oven to 400°.
2. Heat the grits cakes in the oven for 10 minutes. Season the shrimp with coarse sea salt on both sides and grill, turning once, until they are just cooked and have lost their translucence.
3. Transfer the grits cakes to plates. Toss the greens in some of the vinaigrette and season. Arrange a small salad on top of each cake. Remove the shrimp from the skewers and arrange around the cakes, with their tails pointing up. Drizzle some of the vinaigrette over the shrimp and on the plates. Sprinkle with the country ham and thyme. Serve immediately.

Note: If you have two ovens, you can broil the shrimp in one, rather than grilling it, while you heat the grits cakes in the other.

Shrimp Chiles Rellenos with Chipotle-Tomato Vinaigrette & Avocado Salsa

SERVES 8

In August and September of each year, Peregrine Farm chiles start flooding into our farmers' market in a wondrous range of varieties and colors. We always have a relleno on the menu at that time, although the fillings vary from crab to duck to lamb to shrimp. The variation presented in this recipe has always proved to be a crowd-pleaser and encourages advance preparation; the last-minute frying requires only a few minutes.

Look for poblano chiles that are uniform in size, fairly squat in conformation, and not too convoluted to facilitate ease in peeling. If you can't find fresh poblanos, large Anaheim chiles may be used, although they tend to be milder and not as deeply flavored.

INGREDIENTS FOR THE FILLING

2 tablespoons olive oil

½ pound shrimp, peeled and deveined

1 egg

6 ounces whole milk ricotta cheese

zest of 1 lime, grated

juice of 1 lime

1–2 serrano chiles, minced, with seeds

¼ cup diced red bell pepper

¼ cup diced yellow bell pepper

1 fresh pasilla chile, seeded and minced (optional)

1 tablespoon chile spice blend (page 244)

⅔ cup grated Monterey Jack cheese

⅓ cup chopped cilantro

2 tablespoons roasted garlic purée (page 245)

¼ cup Parmesan cheese, grated

salt and black pepper to taste

INGREDIENTS FOR THE CHILES

8 poblano chiles (about 3 ounces each)

2 egg yolks

½ cup heavy cream

1 cup coarse yellow cornmeal

1 teaspoon chile spice blend (page 244)

1 teaspoon dried oregano

salt to taste

peanut oil for deep-frying

INGREDIENTS FOR THE VINAIGRETTE

4 ripe roma tomatoes

4 cloves garlic, unpeeled

1–2 chipotles in adobo sauce, seeded if desired

¼ cup fresh lime juice

¼ cup hot chicken stock

¼ cup olive oil

2 tablespoons fresh oregano, chopped

2 tablespoons cilantro, chopped

salt and black pepper to taste

INGREDIENTS FOR THE SALSA

2 tablespoons red onion, finely diced

2 tablespoons lime juice

2 cloves garlic, minced

2 serrano chiles (or 1 jalapeño), seeded and minced

½ cup tomatillo, cut into small dice

1 firm, ripe avocado, cut into small dice

2 tablespoons olive oil

2 tablespoons cilantro, chopped

salt to taste

PREPARATION FOR THE FILLING

1. Heat the olive oil in a skillet over medium heat. Add the shrimp and season; cook, stirring, until they turn pink and lose their translucent look. Do not overcook. Transfer to a plate, cool, and cut into ½-inch pieces.

2. In a large bowl, combine the egg and ricotta; mix well. Stir in the remaining filling ingredients, season, and fold in the cooked shrimp. Adjust the seasoning with additional lime juice or chile spice if desired. Reserve, refrigerated.

PREPARATION FOR THE CHILES

1. Over an open flame, or under the broiler, char the chiles until they are blistered and blackened, turning often. Transfer to a bowl of ice water to arrest the cooking and preserve the deep green color of the chiles. Peel the blistered skins from the chiles.

2. Using a sharp paring knife, make an incision in each chile from the shoulder two-thirds of the way down to the tip. Using the knife, carefully cut the seed pod from the interior and remove as much of the seeds and membrane as possible. Try to keep the chile intact, but don't panic if you make a small tear.

3. Using a pastry bag or a spoon, fill the chiles with the shrimp mixture but do not overstuff them: the sides of the incision should just meet.

4. In a bowl, whisk the egg yolks and cream together. Combine the cornmeal, chile spice blend, oregano, and salt in a flat baking pan.

5. Dip each chile in the egg mixture and then roll in the cornmeal mixture to coat. Set aside until all the chiles are coated; refrigerate until ready to fry. Reserve the remaining cornmeal mixture.

PREPARATION FOR THE VINAIGRETTE

1. Heat a cast-iron or heavy steel skillet over medium-high heat. Add the tomatoes and garlic and char them, turning often, until blackened. Cool slightly, then peel and seed the tomato; peel the garlic cloves.

2. Transfer the tomatoes and garlic to a blender. Add the chipotle(s) and lime juice and purée. Add the hot chicken stock (or hot water) and, with the blender running, drizzle in olive oil to emulsify. Add the herbs; season with salt and pepper. Adjust the acidity with additional lime juice, as necessary. Set aside at room temperature.

PREPARATION FOR THE SALSA

In a medium stainless bowl, combine the red onion and lime juice; macerate 5 minutes. Add the garlic, chiles, and tomatillo, and then carefully fold in the avocado, olive oil, and cilantro. Season to taste with salt, press the avocado pit down into the salsa, and cover with plastic film, pressing the film down onto surface of the salsa to inhibit oxidation. Set aside at room temperature.

ASSEMBLY

1. Heat peanut oil to 350° in a deep fryer or large heavy kettle. Remove the chiles from the refrigerator, roll again in the reserved cornmeal mixture, and shake off excess. Deep-fry, in batches if necessary, until they are a rich, golden brown and crisp. Keep warm in a slow oven while frying the remaining chiles.

2. Divide the tomato vinaigrette onto 8 plates; drizzle in a random pattern for visual interest. Place a chile on each plate. Remove the avocado pit from the salsa and spoon salsa over and around each chile. Serve immediately.

Pork & Crawfish Potsticker Dumplings with Spicy Cajun Cream

SERVES 6

We were invited to dinner at a private home in Greensboro where Hugh Carpenter was the featured guest. Carpenter is a chef, teacher, and cookbook author who is one of the originators of intelligent fusion cooking. His utilization of American ingredients and Asian technique for salmon potstickers provided the inspiration for this dish, one we have served often to delighted guests.

INGREDIENTS FOR THE POTSTICKER FILLING

2 bunches fresh spinach, stemmed and washed
(or 10 ounces frozen chopped spinach, defrosted)

6 ounces shiitake mushrooms, stemmed and sliced

2 tablespoons ginger, peeled and minced fine

2 tablespoons garlic, minced fine

8 ounces cleaned, cooked crawfish tail meat (or 8 ounces raw, fresh, peeled shrimp), reserved from spicy Cajun cream preparation (see below)

4 ounces lean ground pork

1 tablespoon Chinese chile paste with garlic (available at Oriental markets), or more to taste

2 tablespoons mushroom soy sauce (available at Oriental markets)

4 tablespoons sesame oil, divided

salt and black pepper to taste

1 package fresh dumpling wrappers (or frozen wrappers, defrosted)

PREPARATION

1. In a large sauté pan, heat 2 tablespoons sesame oil until shimmering. Stir-fry the spinach until wilted; drain, cool, and chop coarsely.

2. In a large sauté pan, heat 2 tablespoons sesame oil until shimmering. Stir-fry the shiitakes until crisp and golden. Add the ginger and garlic, and sauté 30 seconds. Turn into a large bowl and cool.

3. Cut each crawfish into 2 or 3 pieces. Add the crawfish (or shrimp, if that's what you're using), pork, spinach, and all the remaining ingredients to the bowl containing the shiitakes and toss to combine. To test the seasoning of the filling, form one small patty and cook it in a sauté pan until the pork is cooked through. Taste for seasoning, adding more chile paste, soy sauce, salt, or pepper as needed.

4. Lay one dumpling wrapper on a dry surface. Place 1 ½ tablespoons of filling in the center and moisten the perimeter of the wrapper with water. Pull the edges of the wrapper up around the filling and crimp decoratively to form an open-top, "shu-mai" style dumpling. Place on a cookie sheet and continue with the remaining wrappers and filling. Yields about 18 dumplings.

5. Refrigerate the dumplings, covered, up to 24 hours, or freeze up to 1 week.

INGREDIENTS FOR THE SALAD

½ pound spicy lettuces (mizzuna, red mustard, tatsoi, spinach)

2 dozen fresh snow peas, trimmed

3 tablespoons rice wine vinegar

1 tablespoon mushroom soy sauce

¼ cup peanut oil

2 tablespoons sesame oil

PREPARATION

1. Wash the lettuces; dry them, reserve, and refrigerate.

2. Blanch the snow peas in boiling salted water. Cool in ice water, drain, and reserve.

3. Make a vinaigrette by combining the remaining ingredients and reserve.

INGREDIENTS FOR THE SPICY CAJUN CREAM

2 pounds fresh crawfish, cooked; reserve 6 whole crawfish in the shell as garnish;
peel and devein all the remaining crawfish for dumpling filling and reserve the
shells. (If you are using shrimp, you will need 12 ounces fresh shrimp in the
shell; peel and devein for the dumpling filling and reserve the shells.)

2 cups homemade chicken stock

10 ounces bottled clam juice

1 cup white wine

2 tablespoons peanut oil

4 ounces onion, finely diced

2 ounces red bell pepper, finely diced

2 ounces green bell pepper, finely diced

2 ounces celery, finely diced

1 tablespoon garlic, minced

1 fresh bay leaf

pinch cayenne pepper (or more to taste)

¼ cup rice wine vinegar

½ cup heavy cream

salt, black pepper, and Tabasco to taste

PREPARATION

1. Combine the reserved crawfish (or shrimp) shells, chicken stock, clam juice,
   and wine in a saucepan. Bring to a boil, reduce to simmer, and cook 20 minutes.
   Strain, pressing on the shells.

2. In the peanut oil, over medium heat, cook the onion, peppers, and celery until
   softened. Add the garlic, bay leaf, and cayenne and cook 1 minute. Add the rice
   wine vinegar and bring to a boil. Add the shellfish stock, bring to a boil, and
   reduce by a quarter. Add the cream, bring to a simmer, and season with salt,
   pepper, and Tabasco; remove the bay leaf. Cool and reserve. Refrigerate if not
   using immediately.

INGREDIENTS FOR THE GARNISH AND ASSEMBLY

¼ cup peanut oil

¼ cup tomato concassé (page 237)

3 scallions, trimmed and sliced thin on the bias

ASSEMBLY AND PRESENTATION

1. Toss the lettuces and snow peas in the vinaigrette and arrange on 6 room-
   temperature plates.

2. Divide the peanut oil between 2 large nonstick pans and heat over medium-high
   heat. Add the dumplings, open-side up, to the pans and brown on the bottoms
   until crisp and deep golden brown. Stir the sauce well and carefully add it to the
   pans. Reduce the heat to medium-low, cover with a lid, and steam the dumplings
   for 2 minutes until hot and cooked through.

3. Place 3 dumplings on each plate around the salad. Divide the sauce, spooning
   over each dumpling, and garnish with a whole crawfish, tomato concassé, and
   scallions. Serve.

Pickled Shrimp with Crab & Pepper Slaw & Smoked Tomato Remoulade

SERVES 8 TO 10

Pickled shrimp are an old-fashioned, Down East standby, piquant and briny at the same time. Served with this wonderful, slightly smoky lump crab slaw, they make a down-home yet distinctive starter for a fancy dinner, or they can be offered on their own with cocktails. Plan to make the shrimp at least 2 days ahead of time; they will keep for a month or longer refrigerated.

INGREDIENTS FOR THE SHRIMP

2 pounds shrimp (26–30 count), cooked (see page 234),
  then shelled and deveined
6 ounces Vidalia or red onion, peeled and sliced paper-thin
2 lemons, sliced thin and seeded
1–2 dried cayenne chile peppers, broken into pieces
½ cup capers, drained
8 cloves garlic, peeled and lightly crushed
6 bay leaves, fresh if available

INGREDIENTS FOR THE MARINADE

1 cup champagne vinegar or tarragon vinegar
½ cup water
¼ cup whole coriander seeds
1 tablespoon whole mustard seeds
1 tablespoon fennel seeds
1 teaspoon allspice berries
4 slices fresh ginger
salt to taste
1 cup olive oil

PREPARATION

1. Combine the marinade ingredients except olive oil in a nonreactive saucepan. Bring to a boil and simmer gently for 10 minutes. Adjust the salt, cool, and add olive oil.
2. In 2 1-quart jars, pack the cooked shrimp, onion, lemon slices, chiles, capers, garlic, and bay leaves in alternating layers. Divide the marinade between the jars, seal, and refrigerate for 48 hours, or up to a month, turning the jars upside down occasionally to distribute the marinade. Keep refrigerated.

INGREDIENTS FOR THE CRAB AND PEPPER SLAW

½ medium green cabbage (we prefer Early Jersey Wakefield cabbage),
  cored and cut crosswise into fine julienne (about 4 cups)
1 red bell pepper, cored, seeded, and julienned
1 yellow bell pepper, cored, seeded, and julienned
1 green bell pepper, cored, seeded, and julienned

2 carrots, peeled and grated

1 cup smoked tomato remoulade (see below)

lemon juice to taste

salt, black pepper, and Tabasco to taste

1 pound lump crabmeat, picked over for shells

PREPARATION

1. Combine the cabbage, peppers, and carrots in a large stainless bowl. Add 1 cup of the remoulade and fold in to combine. Adjust the seasoning with lemon juice, salt, pepper, and Tabasco. The slaw should be slightly acidic to balance the sweetness of the vegetables and crabmeat. Gently fold in the crabmeat so as not to break up lumps.

2. Refrigerate 1 to 4 hours to allow the flavors to meld. Toss gently again before serving.

INGREDIENTS FOR THE REMOULADE

Yield: approximately 1 ½ cups

¼ cup shallots, minced

¼ cup tarragon vinegar

½ cup white wine

2 tablespoons roasted garlic purée (page 245)

2 tablespoons smoked tomato purée (page 238), or more to taste

1 egg yolk, at room temperature

½ cup olive oil

2 tablespoons capers, drained and chopped

2 tablespoons finely chopped cornichons

2 tablespoons chopped flat-leaf parsley

1 tablespoon chopped tarragon

½ teaspoon Tabasco, or more to taste

lemon juice, salt, and black pepper to taste

PREPARATION

1. Combine the shallots, vinegar, and wine in a small nonreactive saucepan. Bring to a boil and simmer until reduced to about 3 tablespoons. Cool.
2. In the bowl of a food processor (or by hand in a stainless steel bowl), combine the shallot reduction, roasted garlic purée, smoked tomato purée, and egg yolk. Pulse to combine. With the machine running, add the olive oil in a fine stream to emulsify. Transfer to a stainless steel bowl, using a plastic spatula.
3. Fold in the capers, cornichons, and herbs. Season to taste with Tabasco, salt, pepper, and more smoked tomato purée if desired. Adjust the acidity with lemon juice. Keeps, refrigerated, up to 3 days.

ASSEMBLY AND PRESENTATION

1. Remove the shrimp from the pickle and brush off any extraneous bits of marinade clinging to them. Discard the marinade.
2. Gently toss the slaw and divide between cool plates, mounding in the center. Divide shrimp around the slaw, arranging attractively, and spoon a little of the reserved remoulade onto the shrimp. Garnish with some sliced scallions or flat-leaf parsley leaves and serve immediately.

Hot Smoked (or Grilled) Oysters
with Preserved Lemon & Caviar

SERVES 4 TO 6 REGULAR PEOPLE, OR 2 FANATICS

We love oysters in every way, shape, or form, but this is a particularly elegant and sublime presentation. Served warm straight off the grill, lightly smoked, or chilled, they make an outstanding beginning to a special meal.

We prefer Atlantic varieties for their larger, flatter shape, which lends itself to this presentation; we also find them to be more briny in taste, which is a personal preference.

INGREDIENTS

- 2 dozen Malpeque, bluepoint, Chincoteague, Maine belon, or other medium-to-large Atlantic oysters, in the shell, washed
- ½ cup crème fraîche (or clabbered cream, available from Egg Farm Dairy [see Sources])
- ½ cup preserved lemon (see below), cut into fine dice
- 2 ounces sevruga caviar
- ¼ cup snipped chives or chervil
- 2 pounds rock salt or stone-ground grits

PREPARATION

1. Make preserved lemons (see below). These should be made 1 to 2 weeks in advance. Cut into fine dice.
2. Light the grill or smoker. Arrange the oysters on a rack with their flat side up. If smoking the oysters, add smoked wood chips to the fire and cover for 5 minutes to build up smoke. Place the rack with the oysters on the grill or smoker and cook over medium-high heat until the top shells of the oysters pop. Remove the oysters from the rack *as soon as the shells open* to avoid overcooking; place on a sheet pan layered with rock salt to stabilize the oysters. They may be chilled at this point or served warm.
3. To serve: with an oyster knife, remove the top shell, being careful not to spill any juices. Release the bottom muscle with the knife and place on a serving platter layered with rock salt or coarse grits. Top each oyster with ¼ teaspoon of crème fraîche, ¼ teaspoon of preserved lemon, and ¼ teaspoon of caviar. Sprinkle with the snipped chives or chervil.

INGREDIENTS FOR PRESERVED LEMONS

- 5 lemons
- ½ cup sugar
- 1 tablespoon salt
- ¾ cup water
- 1 bay leaf

PREPARATION

1. Cut each lemon into 16 thin wedges and remove the seeds. Blanch in boiling water for 1 minute. Drain and then cool in ice water. Drain thoroughly.

2. Combine the sugar, salt, water, and bay leaf in a saucepan. Bring to a boil, add the lemons, and reduce the heat to medium-low. Simmer for 10 minutes, until the lemons are tender. Cool in the syrup, then store in the refrigerator.
3. To use, remove the number of lemons needed from the syrup, remove and discard the flesh, and cut the peel into the desired shape.
4. Will keep indefinitely, covered and refrigerated.

Fried Oysters on Creamy Winter Succotash with Barbecue Vinaigrette

SERVES 4 TO 6

Ahhh, fried oysters. . . . We do them so many different ways, it's difficult to choose one dish. This one commingles some of the aspects we like best: crunchy, briny, salty, creamy, tangy, a little bit spicy. Plus it's an opportunity to sneak some hominy by an unsuspecting victim who's loudly proclaimed his disdain for that lowly grain.

Have everything ready before you fry your oysters; the key to success is for them to be hot and GBD (golden brown and delicious).

INGREDIENTS FOR THE OYSTERS

    1 ½ pints shucked oysters, drained, with liquor reserved
    1 cup coarse stone-ground cornmeal
    ½ cup flour
    ¼ teaspoon cayenne pepper
    ¼ teaspoon freshly ground black pepper
    ½ teaspoon salt
    peanut oil for frying

INGREDIENTS FOR THE SUCCOTASH

    2 tablespoons peanut oil
    3 ounces country ham, cut into small dice
    ¼ cup fennel bulb, cut into small dice
    ¼ cup carrot, cut into small dice
    ½ cup onion, cut into small dice
    ¼ cup red bell pepper, cut into small dice
    1 tablespoon minced garlic
    pinch crushed red pepper flakes
    1 bay leaf
    1 pint fresh or frozen baby lima beans
    chicken stock as needed
    salt and black pepper to taste
    1 cup white hominy, drained and rinsed
    ¾ cup heavy cream
    1 teaspoon thyme leaves
    1 tablespoon parsley, chopped

cider vinegar to taste

1 cup arugula leaves, coarsely chopped

¼ cup chopped scallions

INGREDIENTS FOR THE BARBECUE VINAIGRETTE

¼ cup cider vinegar

2 tablespoons honey

1 tablespoon tamarind concentrate (available at Oriental markets)

pinch crushed red pepper flakes

¼ cup reserved oyster liquor, strained

2 tablespoons roasted garlic purée (page 245)

2 tablespoons tomato paste

¼ cup peanut oil

salt, black pepper, and Tabasco to taste

PREPARATION FOR THE SUCCOTASH

1. In a saucepot, heat the oil over medium heat and cook the country ham until lightly browned. Remove the ham, leaving the renderings in the pan. Add the fennel, carrot, onion, and pepper and cook over medium heat until softened and starting to caramelize. Add the garlic, red pepper flakes, and bay leaf; cook 1 minute.

2. Add the lima beans and enough chicken stock to barely cover. Bring to a simmer and cook until the limas are just tender. Set aside.

3. While the limas are cooking, combine the hominy and cream in a small saucepan, bring to a boil, and simmer, stirring occasionally, until the cream is reduced and thickened. Stir into the limas and adjust the seasoning. Reserve.

PREPARATION FOR THE VINAIGRETTE

1. Combine the vinegar, honey, tamarind, red pepper flakes, and oyster liquor in a small saucepan. Bring to a boil and simmer for 5 minutes. Transfer to a blender.

2. Add the roasted garlic purée and tomato paste to the warm ingredients and blend to combine. With the blender running, drizzle in peanut oil to emulsify. Season and set aside at room temperature.

PREPARATION FOR THE OYSTERS

1. Combine the cornmeal, flour, cayenne, salt, and black pepper in a bowl. Toss the oysters in the dredging mixture to coat.

2. Heat peanut oil to a depth of 3 to 4 inches in a heavy pot or deep fryer at 350° (use a deep-frying thermometer).

3. Warm the succotash over low heat. Add the thyme and parsley, and salt, pepper, and vinegar to taste, and stir in the country ham and arugula. Keep warm.

4. Remove the oysters from the dredge, shaking off excess. Fry, in batches if necessary, until crisp. Drain on brown paper bags.

5. Divide the succotash between hot bowls. Pile fried oysters on top of the succotash and spoon barbecue vinaigrette around. Sprinkle with chopped scallions and serve immediately.

Crab Cakes with Sauce Diable & Corn Relish Salad

YIELDS 12 CRAB CAKES, SERVING 6 AS A FIRST COURSE

We have served numerous variations of crab cakes at the restaurant, but they have all been founded on this basic recipe. You can change the peppers, add herbs, or spice the crab cakes differently, but we like the balance of the sweet crabmeat, the piquant "devil's" sauce, and the crunch of the corn relish in the arugula salad.

Be careful when making the crab cake mixture to handle it gently and minimally. If you're going to spend the money for lump crabmeat, you want to preserve those sweet morsels.

INGREDIENTS FOR THE CRAB CAKES

  2 eggs
  2 tablespoons lemon juice
  2 tablespoons lime juice
  ½ cup red bell pepper, cut into fine dice
  ½ cup yellow bell pepper, cut into fine dice
  1 pound lump or jumbo lump crabmeat, picked over for shells
  1 teaspoon Worcestershire sauce
  Tabasco to taste
  approximately ¾ cup dried bread crumbs (or more if needed)
  salt and black pepper to taste
  clarified butter (page 243)

INGREDIENTS FOR THE SAUCE DIABLE

  ½ cup sour cream
  2 tablespoons Dijon mustard
  2 tablespoons coarse-grain mustard
  2 tablespoons lemon juice (or more, to taste)
  pinch cayenne pepper
  1 jalapeño, seeded and minced
  2 tablespoons parsley, chopped
  1 tablespoon tarragon, chopped
  salt and black pepper to taste

INGREDIENTS FOR THE SALAD

  ½ small red onion, sliced paper-thin (about ¼ cup)
  ¼ cup Iowa corn relish (page 179), with juices
  1 pickled chipotle (from the corn relish, optional), seeded and minced
  3 tablespoons fruity olive oil
  1 ½ cups arugula, washed and stemmed
  salt and black pepper to taste
  2 tablespoons chives, cut into ½-inch lengths

1. Combine the eggs, juices, and diced peppers in a mixing bowl. With a rubber spatula, or your hand, gently fold in the crabmeat. Add the Worcestershire, Tabasco, and bread crumbs and season with salt and pepper. You may have to add a few more bread crumbs so that the mixture holds together, but be careful—the mixture should be moist.

2. Using a 1½-inch biscuit cutter as a mold, divide the mixture into 12 equal cakes, pressing firmly to form even shapes. Refrigerate for 30 minutes, or up to 4 hours.

3. Make the sauce. Whisk the sour cream, mustards, and lemon juice together in a bowl. Stir in the cayenne, jalapeño, and herbs. Season and reserve.

4. Make the vinaigrette. Combine the red onion, corn relish, (optional) chipotle, and olive oil. Season and set aside.

5. Heat 1 or 2 large skillets over medium-high heat. Add the clarified butter and the crab cakes and lower the heat to medium. Cook 2 minutes, or until golden brown. Turn gently and cook on the second side 1 to 2 minutes, until browned and heated through.

6. Spoon sauce onto 6 plates and spread in a circle. Place 2 crab cakes on each plate. Toss the arugula with the corn relish vinaigrette; season with salt and pepper. Divide the salad between the plates, placing it between the crab cakes on each, and sprinkle with chives. Serve immediately.

Black Bass Sashimi with Warm Thai "Shrimp" Vinaigrette

SERVES 4 AS A FIRST COURSE

Inspired by ethnic restaurant treks down Geary Boulevard in San Francisco, this essentially raw fish presentation is dependent on your source for fresh seafood. Catch it yourself or trust your fishmonger. You may substitute snapper or Spanish mackeral for the bass, but, whatever fish you use, wait to cut it until the last moment.

We prepare some versions of this dish with poached lobster and chanterelle salad but accompany this Thai-influenced version with a salad of shaved fennel, radishes, and tiny red mustard leaves.

INGREDIENTS

12 ounces impeccably fresh black sea bass, skin on, boneless

1 teaspoon garlic, minced

1 teaspoon ginger, minced

2 ounces shrimp shells (or ½ teaspoon Thai shrimp paste)

2 tablespoons peanut oil

1 serrano chile, seeded if desired, and minced

1 teaspoon tamarind concentrate (available at Oriental markets)

pinch saffron

1 roma tomato, chopped

2 tablespoons rice wine vinegar

¼ cup lime juice

¼ cup white port

1 cup chicken stock

2 fresh kaffir lime leaves and 1 stalk lemongrass, minced (optional)

1 ripe red serrano chile, seeded and minced

1 tablespoon shallot, diced fine

3 tablespoons extra virgin sesame oil (do not use toasted sesame oil; if necessary, substitute safflower or peanut oil instead)

fish sauce to taste

sea salt

2 tablespoons mint, cut into chiffonade (see note)

1 tablespoon sesame seeds, lightly toasted

¼ cup scallions, sliced fine on the bias

PREPARATION

1. In a small saucepan, cook the garlic, ginger, and shrimp shells in oil until aromatic. Add the chile, tamarind, saffron, and tomato; cook 1 minute. Add the vinegar, lime juice, and white port; bring to a boil and cook 2 minutes. Add the stock and the (optional) lime leaves and lemongrass, bring to a simmer, and reduce by half.

2. Put the red serrano chile and shallots in a heat-proof container. Strain the shrimp reduction onto the chile-shallot mixture, pressing on the solids to extract all the shrimp and tomato juices. Cool, then whisk in the sesame oil and fish sauce to taste.

3. Using a thin-blade, razor-sharp knife, cut wafer-thin slices of the bass on a steep bias against the skin. Divide slices of bass in a flower petal fashion on 4 heat-proof plates. Season with ground sea salt.

4. Heat the vinaigrette over medium heat until just simmering. Immediately add the mint and pour the hot vinaigrette over the slices of fish. Sprinkle with sesame seeds and scallions and serve immediately.

Note: To cut an herb into chiffonade, stack several leaves on top of each other. Roll the herb stack into a tight cigar and cut crosswise into fine strips.

Crisp Peppered Quail with Country Ham & Spicy Crawfish Hominy

SERVES 6 AS A FIRST COURSE

When *Food & Wine* sent its anonymous diner to evaluate the restaurant for the magazine's Best New Chefs designation, this is the dish that apparently turned the diner on. We had created the dish for the first Salute to Southern Chefs in Charleston and just happened to be testing it on the menu the night the *Food & Wine* representative came to the Grill. Luck? Or great flavors that work well together? Doesn't matter—a Yankee food writer ate hominy and loved it.

If you're unable to acquire live crawfish, fresh or frozen peeled tail meat is available from your fishmonger.

INGREDIENTS FOR THE QUAIL

6 semiboneless quail (4–5 ounces each)
2 tablespoons bourbon
1 tablespoon molasses
½ teaspoon coarsely ground black pepper
3 tablespoons fresh thyme, divided
½ cup peanut oil, divided

INGREDIENTS FOR THE HOMINY

1½ pounds live crawfish, cleaned (or ¼ pound fresh or frozen peeled tail meat)
3 ounces thinly sliced country ham, trimmed of fat and cut into julienne strips
½ cup onion, finely diced
¼ cup celery rib, peeled and finely diced
⅓ cup red bell pepper, finely diced
⅓ cup green bell pepper, finely diced
1 tablespoon minced garlic
½ teaspoon freshly ground black pepper

½ teaspoon fennel seeds, ground

½ teaspoon paprika

¼ teaspoon cayenne pepper

2 cups tomato-crawfish stock (see recipe below) or chicken stock

1 16-ounce can cooked hominy, drained and rinsed in cold water

salt and black pepper

1 medium tomato, peeled, seeded, and cut into ¼-inch dice

3 tablespoons unsalted butter

INGREDIENTS FOR THE GARNISH

2 scallions, thinly sliced on the diagonal

6 whole crawfish (reserved from hominy preparation)

a few sprigs fresh thyme

PREPARATION

1. Make an incision through the skin at the base of each quail breast and tuck in the legs. In a large, shallow dish, combine the bourbon, molasses, coarsely ground pepper, 1 tablespoon of the thyme, and ¼ cup of the peanut oil. Add the quail and stir to coat. Cover and marinate in the refrigerator for at least 4 hours, turning occasionally.

2. Cook the crawfish in a large pot of salted boiling water until they are bright red, about 5 minutes. Drain and plunge the crawfish into ice water. Peel and devein the crawfish, reserving 6 whole ones for garnish. Reserve the crawfish shells for the stock.

3. Heat the remaining ¼ cup of peanut oil in a large skillet. Add the country ham and cook over high heat, stirring, until crisp, about 2 minutes. Transfer to paper towels to drain. Add the onion, celery, and red and green bell peppers to the skillet and cook over moderately low heat until softened, about 5 minutes. Add the garlic, freshly ground black pepper, ground fennel seeds, paprika, and cayenne and cook for 1 minute.

4. Add the tomato-crawfish stock to the skillet and bring to a boil over high heat. Lower the heat and simmer until reduced by a third, about 10 minutes. Add the hominy and cook until heated through; season with salt and pepper to taste. (The recipe can be prepared up to this point as far as 1 day ahead. Cover and refrigerate the quail, crawfish, ham, and hominy separately.)

5. Light the grill or preheat the broiler. Reheat the hominy if necessary. Stir in the crawfish, ham, diced tomato, and the remaining 2 tablespoons thyme and cook over moderate heat until just warmed through. Stir in the butter and keep warm.

6. Season the quail with salt and pepper and grill skin-side down for 2 minutes. Turn and continue grilling until the skin is crisp and the meat is pink, 2 to 3 minutes longer.

7. To serve: spoon the hominy onto 6 plates and place a quail on top of each serving. Sprinkle on the sliced scallions and garnish each plate with a whole crawfish and thyme sprigs.

reserved crawfish shells

½ cup olive oil

1 pound large plum tomatoes, coarsely chopped

2 bay leaves

1 cup dry white wine

1 quart chicken stock

PREPARATION

1. Crush the crawfish shells by wrapping them in a towel and pounding with a mallet; or you may use a food processor. Heat the olive oil over medium-high heat; add the shells and cook, stirring, for 5 minutes.

2. Add the tomatoes, bay leaves, and wine, stirring to scrape all bits and pieces from the bottom of the pot.

3. Add the chicken stock, bring to a simmer, and cook until reduced to 2 cups, about 30 minutes. Strain, pressing the solids to extract as much liquid as possible, cool, and refrigerate for up to 24 hours.

Roast Saddle of Rabbit Wrapped in Country Ham on Warm Brunswick Stew & Wild Watercress Salad

SERVES 8 AS A FIRST COURSE

This is a fairly complicated first course we created for a benefit dinner called Salute to Southern Chefs in Charleston. We wanted to integrate the flavors of Brunswick stew, often made with rabbit in North Carolina's western Piedmont, into a complex and stylish presentation.

Fresh rabbit is getting to be more readily available as consumers become attuned to its low fat content and high degree of flavor. You may have to special order fresh rabbit loins from your butcher, but we recommend avoiding frozen ones at all costs.

INGREDIENTS FOR THE RABBIT

2 whole rabbit saddles, boned and silverskin removed,
  with bones, tenderloins, and flanks reserved

1 teaspoon fresh thyme leaves

1 tablespoon sage leaves, chopped

1 tablespoon parsley leaves, chopped

2 teaspoons roasted garlic purée (page 245)

1 tablespoon olive oil + olive oil for searing

salt and freshly ground black pepper

2 ounces country ham, sliced paper-thin and closely trimmed of fat
  (you may substitute Spanish serrano ham, prosciutto, or Parma ham)

INGREDIENTS FOR THE JUICE

reserved rabbit bones and flanks

2 tablespoons olive oil

2 tablespoons garlic, minced

4 shallots, minced (¼ cup)

½ teaspoon crushed red pepper flakes,
  or 1 small dried cayenne chile pepper, crushed

2 tablespoons sourwood honey

¼ cup sage vinegar (or cider vinegar)

1 cup white wine

2 cups rabbit stock (or roasted chicken stock [page 228])

2 thyme branches

2 sage branches

salt and freshly ground black pepper

INGREDIENTS FOR THE SALAD

2 tablespoons olive oil

2 shallots, peeled and sliced thin crosswise

6 ounces baby lima beans or speckled butterbeans (fresh or frozen)

1 cup rabbit or chicken stock

½ cup fresh corn kernels

2 bunches wild or cultivated watercress, trimmed,
  washed, and dried, then reserved

3 ounces Red Bliss or Yukon Gold potatoes, cut into ¼-inch dice,
  poached in salted water until tender, drained, and reserved

1 teaspoon thyme leaves

1 teaspoon sage leaves, chopped

1 tablespoon parsley leaves, chopped

salt and freshly ground black pepper

INGREDIENTS FOR THE VINAIGRETTE

1 teaspoon garlic, minced

2 tablespoons sourwood honey

¼ cup sage vinegar (or cider vinegar)

½ cup oven-dried tomatoes (page 237), coarsely chopped
  (or substitute sun-dried tomatoes)

¼ cup olive oil (or peanut oil)

salt and freshly ground black pepper

INGREDIENTS FOR THE GARNISH

3 tablespoons sage oil (page 241)

8 fresh sage sprays

PREPARATION

1. Assemble the rabbit loins. Combine the herbs, roasted garlic purée, and olive oil. Season the loins with salt and pepper. Heat oil in a steel or cast-iron pan, and sear the loins over medium heat until lightly browned; keep rare. Remove from heat and cool. Spread the herb mixture on the loins, wrap in country ham in spiral fashion, and refrigerate until 20 to 30 minutes before cooking.

2. Make the rabbit juice. In a 2- or 3-quart heavy-bottomed saucepan, heat the

olive oil over medium heat. Add the bones and flanks and cook over medium heat until well browned. Add the garlic, shallots, and red pepper flakes and cook for 1 to 2 minutes. Stir in the honey, vinegar, and wine. Add the rabbit (or roasted chicken) stock and bring to a boil. Reduce to a simmer and reduce the volume by half. Strain into a 1-quart saucepan. Bring to a boil, then reduce to a simmer. Cook until reduced to 4 ounces. Add the thyme and sage and steep for 10 minutes. Strain, season, and keep warm.

3. Make the salad. In a 1-quart heavy-bottomed saucepan, heat the olive oil over medium heat. Add the shallots, reduce the heat to low, and cook until the shallots are softened but not browned. Add the limas and stock, bring to a boil, reduce the heat to medium-low, and simmer until the beans are tender. Stir in the corn, cook 1 minute, and season. Cool and reserve. Drain excess liquid—this should be fluid but not soupy.

4. Make the vinaigrette. Combine the garlic, honey, and vinegar. Stir in the oven-dried tomatoes and olive oil. Season to taste. Reserve.

5. Prepare the rabbit loins. Preheat oven to 400°. Heat a large sauté pan over medium-high heat. Add 2 tablespoons olive oil and sear the loins on all sides, about 1½ to 2 minutes. Put the pan in the oven for 2 minutes longer. Remove from the oven, transfer to a cutting board, and keep warm.

6. Assembly. Place the watercress in a large stainless steel bowl. Warm the butterbeans and corn over medium heat, add the potatoes, and stir in the herbs and vinaigrette. Check the seasoning. Pour over the watercress, toss, and divide between 8 warm plates. Slice the rabbit loins crosswise into 4 or 5 pieces and arrange around the salad on each plate. Drizzle the juice over the loins and onto the plate. Drizzle on sage oil and garnish with a sage spray.

entrées

Roasted Mint-&-Garlic-Rubbed Fresh Ham with
  Salsa Verde & Luxe Macaroni & Cheese

Pan-Fried Pork Chops on Creamy Shrimp
  Hominy

Smoked Pork Tenderloin

Pork Osso Buco with Creole Baked Beans

Herb-Crusted Rack of Pork on Brunswick "Stew"

Beef Shortribs in Barbecued Onion Sauce with
  Grilled Spring Leeks & Roasted Garlic Grits

Grilled Beef Tenderloin in Cabernet Sauce
  with Roquefort & Summer Vegetable
  Chopped Salad

Grilled Lamb Chops with a Ragout of Baby
  Artichokes, Olives, & Oven-Dried Tomatoes

Venison Medallions in Zinfandel–Black Pepper Jus

Rabbit Confit with Marinated Baby Artichokes,
  Newly Dug Potatoes, & Spring Vegetables

Gabriel's Favorite Crispy Parmesan Chicken
  with Lemon & Capers

Simple Roast Chicken with Duck Fat Potatoes

Grilled Quail on Crawfish Jambalaya Risotto
  with Smoked Tomato & Sage Essence

Our Thanksgiving Turkey with
"140" Cloves of Garlic

Pan-Roasted Duck Breast with Sun-Dried
Cherry Conserve

Duck Confit with Barbecued Lentils

Confit Duck Hash with Poached Eggs
& Béarnaise Aioli

Roast Squab with Blackberry Essence
& Carrot-Thyme Spaetzle

Striped Bass with Oyster Stew

Pan-Fried Mountain Rainbow Trout with
Green Tomato & Lime Brown Butter Salsa
on Sweet Potato, Artichoke, & Crawfish Hash

Grilled Tuna with Roasted Eggplant
& Cucumber Vermicelli

Halibut in Sorrel & Lemongrass Nage with
Morels & Spring Onion–Asparagus Fondue

Pan-Seared Red Snapper with Lobster Tomato
Sauce & Gazpacho Garnish

Grilled Sturgeon on Wild Rice Risotto
with Butternuts, Grilled Leeks,
& Cider Reduction

Schoolkids' Flounder with Fish Camp

Beurre Blanc

Salmon Choucroute in Creamy Mustard Sauce

Summer Shell Bean Minestra with

Tomato Bruschetta

Fried Green Tomato Sandwich on Buttermilk

Bread with Arugula, Country Bacon,

& Black Pepper Aioli

Roasted Mint-&-Garlic-Rubbed Fresh Ham with Salsa Verde & Luxe Macaroni & Cheese

SERVES A CROWD

Our friend Louis Osteen, of Louis's in Charleston, used to host a Labor Day weekend barbecue. Inviting a few North Carolina chefs to join the party, and throwing down the barbecue gauntlet, he'd line up a bunch of pig cookers, and a lot of beer, and we'd pretend that we were working. One year, we wanted to avoid having to prove that North Carolina–style pork barbecue is superior in every way to South Carolina's, so we got some green hams and cooked up something entirely different.

Green hams are not rotten hams: "green" refers to a fresh, uncured pork leg. Super juicy and so flavorful, they are a wonderful big-party roast. You can, of course, slow smoke one over hardwood, if you really want to make your company swoon. Leftovers, if there are any, make excellent green chile or taco filling, or can be chopped and tossed with pasta and the same salsa verde.

INGREDIENTS FOR THE HAM

> 1 10-pound fresh ham, close-trimmed
> 2 cups packed mint leaves
> 1 cup packed Italian parsley leaves
> 20 cloves garlic, poached in water until tender
> 6 jalapeños, seeded and stemmed
> ⅔ cup olive oil
> ¼ cup (2 ounces) kosher salt

INGREDIENTS FOR THE SALSA VERDE

> 2 tablespoons chopped garlic
> 1 tablespoon coarsely chopped capers
> 1 teaspoon finely chopped anchovies (optional)
> ½ cup packed Italian parsley leaves
> ½ cup packed basil leaves
> ½ cup packed mint leaves
> zest of 2 lemons, minced
> olive oil, as needed

INGREDIENTS FOR SERVING

> 1 recipe luxe macaroni and cheese (page 159)
> mint sprigs for garnish

PREPARATION FOR THE HAM

> 1. In a food processor, combine the herbs, garlic, and jalapeños. Pulse to chop. Add the oil and salt and then purée. Coat the entire surface of the ham with this mixture and place it on a rack in a roasting pan. Refrigerate for 3 to 4 hours or overnight. Remove from the refrigerator 1½ hours before roasting.

2. Preheat oven to 350°. Roast the ham at 350° for 45 minutes, then reduce the oven temperature to 300° and roast for 20 minutes per pound, or until the internal temperature reaches 155° to 160° (or higher if desired). Cover with foil if the crust begins to darken. Let rest for 30 minutes.

3. Slice the ham against the grain into ⅓-inch slices. Serve on luxe macaroni and cheese. Drizzle with salsa verde. Garnish with mint.

PREPARATION FOR THE SALSA VERDE

Combine the garlic, capers, anchovies, parsley, basil, mint, and lemon zest in a food processor. Pulse to chop. Add the olive oil until the mixture forms a fluid purée. Keeps refrigerated for 24 hours. Serve at room temperature.

Pan-Fried Pork Chops on Creamy Shrimp Hominy

SERVES 4

Native Americans created hominy in order to preserve corn. Dried corn kernels are soaked to remove the husk, traditionally in lye, which acts as a bleaching agent.

Ben's mother used to prepare "smothered" pork chops and serve them with buttered hominy on the side for family suppers. This recipe was created for a *Food & Wine* article on comfort food; it certainly fulfills that qualification. Serve with string beans sautéed with bacon.

INGREDIENTS FOR THE PORK CHOPS

    4 pork T-bone chops (8 ounces each)
    ½ cup flour
    1 teaspoon salt
    1 tablespoon ground black pepper
    1 teaspoon paprika
    ½ teaspoon cayenne pepper
    1 teaspoon dried oregano
    peanut oil
    ¼ cup bourbon
    ¼ cup cider vinegar
    1 cup white wine
    salt and black pepper to taste

PREPARATION

    1. Heat a heavy sauté pan or cast-iron pan over medium heat for 5 minutes. Combine the flour, salt, black pepper, cayenne, paprika, and oregano on a shallow plate. Pat the pork chops dry with paper towels and lightly dredge them in the seasoned flour, shaking off excess.

    2. Add peanut oil to the hot pan to a depth of ¼ inch. Pan-fry the chops for 2 to 3 minutes per side, until nicely browned, and remove from the pan. Pour off excess oil.

3. Off the heat, deglaze the pan with the bourbon and cider vinegar. Return to the heat and bring to a boil; add the wine and pork chops, bring to a simmer and cook, *covered*, over low heat for 8 to 10 minutes, until the chops are cooked to medium. Remove the chops and keep warm. Reduce the braising juices by half, skimming impurities from the top. Season.

INGREDIENTS FOR THE CREAMY SHRIMP HOMINY

1 15-ounce can white hominy, drained, rinsed in cold water, drained, and reserved
1 cup heavy cream
3 tablespoons peanut oil
1 medium onion, cut into fine dice
4 ounces green bell pepper, seeded and cut into fine dice
2 ribs celery, cut into fine dice
1 bay leaf
1 jalapeño, seeded and minced fine (or 1 teaspoon crushed red pepper flakes)
2 tablespoons minced garlic
2 tablespoons oregano, chopped
1 tablespoon thyme leaves
1 cup canned tomatoes, seeded and chopped
¼ cup cider vinegar
2 cups shrimp stock (page 233)
8 ounces shrimp, peeled, split lengthwise, and deveined,
    with shells reserved for stock
salt, black pepper, and Tabasco to taste
1 bunch scallions, green tops only, sliced crosswise into rings for garnish

PREPARATION

1. In a 1-quart saucepan, combine the rinsed hominy and cream; bring to a simmer over medium heat and cook until lightly thickened, about 5 minutes. Reserve.
2. In a heavy-bottomed 3-quart saucepan or rondeau, heat the peanut oil over medium heat. Add the onion, green pepper, and celery; cook until softened but not browned.
3. Add the bay leaf, jalapeño, garlic, herbs, and tomatoes and cook 2 minutes, stirring. Add the vinegar and shrimp stock, bring to a boil, reduce the heat, and simmer gently for 15 minutes. Stir in the hominy cream and return to a simmer.
4. Stir in the shrimp and cook 1 to 2 minutes, until just opaque. Season with salt, black pepper, and Tabasco if desired.

TO SERVE

Divide the shrimp hominy between 4 plates or wide, shallow bowls. Place a chop on each, spoon some pan juices over the chop, and sprinkle with the chopped scallion greens.

Smoked Pork Tenderloin

SERVES 6 TO 8 AS PART OF A BUFFET;
SERVES 4 GENEROUSLY AS AN ENTRÉE

We have probably grilled at least a tractor trailer full of pork tenderloins in our time; we've always smoked them lightly and finished them on the grill, but you may choose to cook them entirely on the smoker.

The marinade lends a faint sweetness that caramelizes on the grill, and the pork is delicious hot or served at room temperature. We like it as part of a Southern buffet with Abundance plum chutney (page 176), bean salad (page 154), and/or sweet potato salad (page 164).

INGREDIENTS

   2 pounds fresh pork tenderloin, trimmed
   ¼ cup bourbon
   2 tablespoons molasses
   1 tablespoon crushed red pepper flakes
   4 cloves garlic, crushed
   2 bay leaves, crushed
   10 sprigs fresh thyme, coarsely chopped
   6 sprigs fresh sage, coarsely chopped
   ¾ cup olive or peanut oil
   salt

PREPARATION

   1. Combine the bourbon and molasses. Add the remaining ingredients and roll the pork in this marinade. Refrigerate 8 hours, or overnight, turning occasionally.
   2. Remove the pork from the marinade, season with salt, and smoke over hickory, cherry, or applewood, basting with the marinade, for 15 to 20 minutes. The pork may then continue to cook on a smoker, be finished on a grill, or be roasted in a 350° oven until it reaches an internal temperature of 145° to 150° degrees. Remove from heat and rest the tenderloin for 10 minutes before slicing. This can be made ahead and refrigerated; bring to room temperature before serving.

Tips on Smoking

We have smoked more pork than anything else in our tenure on Ninth Street, but there's also been salmon, bluefish, sturgeon, and trout on that double-chambered cooker out back—and Vidalia onions, roasted peppers and tomatoes (*lots* of tomatoes), whole beef tenderloins and ribeyes, cowboy steaks and New York strips, oysters and clams, squid and shrimp, ad infinitum. We generally use hardwood charcoal and soaked hickory chips, although we've also used apple and cherry, occasionally persimmon wood, and, in a pinch, dead wood off the pecan trees behind the restaurant.

Usually we're cold-smoking proteins to imbue them with a woodsy aroma and flavor prior to finishing their cooking on the grill or the range. The use of indirect heat and a slow, gentle smoke lets us use that smoke as an additional flavoring component and, frankly, provides us with a link to the generations of hardwood cooks that have preceded us in North Carolina.

Typically, we marinate meats for 6 to 24 hours before giving them a short smoke to flavor them. We'll then finish them on the grill to sear and seal in the juices. Often we brine poultry, such as duck breasts and chickens, because we find the curing process helps them to take the smoke better. We also brine whole trout and salmon filets for 24 hours and then dry them on a rack in the refrigerator to form the "pellicle," a "skin" on the surface of the fish that enhances the absorption of the smoke. Then we'll cold-smoke the fish over a bed of ice so they don't cook during the process.

Vegetables, smoked only briefly, so that they're not overwhelmed, add an interesting component to salsas and ragouts. We've even smoked reconstituted dried fruits to make compotes for terrines and sausages. There are virtually no limitations to what you can smoke as long as you view the process as a seasoning, like salt and pepper: noticeable when it's absent, overwhelming when there's too much.

Whatever you're going to put on your smoker, soak your chips for 12 to 24 hours beforehand so they're steaming and giving off smoke, not burning and producing heat. Let your coals burn down until they're covered with a fine gray ash—"low and slow is the way to go." Always use hardwood charcoal and wood chips so you don't get harsh chemical flavors on your food. Cover the coals with a layer of soaked chips and set the dampers on your smoker (if it has them) to produce a smooth, even draft. If you anticipate a long smoke, such as for a whole turkey, have additional coals and soaked chips ready and waiting, so you don't interrupt the process.

Magnolia Grill sits across the street from the West Durham Fire Station, and our first day of smoking generated quite a response from our neighbors. Now, it's just part of Ninth Street's daily ambience.

Pork Osso Buco with Creole Baked Beans

SERVES 6

Goodness gracious, this is Dixie comfort food! In our quest for Southern interpretations of traditional dishes from other cuisines, we created this take on osso buco Milanese, veal shank with saffron risotto. Technique was the jumping-off point, but all similarities end there. This dish benefits from advance preparation to allow all the deep flavors to marry.

INGREDIENTS FOR THE OSSO BUCO

    6 meaty pork osso buco (see note), 1½–2 inches thick
    ¼ cup molasses
    ¼ cup cider vinegar
    1½ cups white wine
    ½ cup bourbon
    4 bay leaves
    8 cloves garlic, peeled and lightly crushed
    8 sprigs fresh rosemary
    12 sprigs fresh thyme
    1½ teaspoons crushed red pepper flakes
    salt and black pepper
    ¼ cup olive oil
    chicken stock or water

INGREDIENTS FOR THE CREOLE BAKED BEANS

    1 pound small red beans, picked over for debris, stones,
        and broken beans and soaked overnight in cold water
    8 ounces andouille sausage, quartered lengthwise and sliced crosswise
    ¼ cup olive oil
    1 cup onion, cut into small dice
    2 ribs celery, cut into small dice
    1 red bell pepper, cut into small dice
    1 green bell pepper, cut into small dice
    ¼ cup minced garlic
    1 bay leaf
    1 teaspoon crushed red pepper flakes
    1 tablespoon Creole spice blend (page 243)
    3 tablespoons dark brown sugar
    1 tablespoon dry mustard
    1 cup seeded, chopped tomatoes
    ½ pound smoked pork neck bones or 1 large meaty smoked ham hock
    chicken stock (about 1 quart, or more as needed)
    salt
    2 tablespoons chopped oregano
    ½ cup chopped parsley
    cider vinegar to taste

2 cups young red mustard greens or arugula, stemmed and washed

½ cup Iowa corn relish (page 179)

2 tablespoons olive oil

salt and black pepper

2 cups cooked white rice

PREPARATION FOR THE OSSO BUCO

1. Combine the molasses and cider vinegar in a bowl and stir to mix. Add the wine, bourbon, bay leaves, garlic, rosemary, thyme, and red pepper flakes. Mix well and marinate the pork in this mixture, refrigerated, for 24 hours. Turn the pork in the marinade occasionally. Remove from the refrigerator 1 hour before cooking.

2. Preheat oven to 350°. Remove the pork from the marinade, wiping off any excess and season liberally with salt and pepper. Reserve the marinade. Heat a large, heavy skillet over medium-high heat, add the olive oil, and sear the pork on all sides until deeply browned.

3. Transfer to a deep ovenproof baking or roasting pan large enough to hold the pork in one layer. Pour the marinade over the pork and add chicken stock or water to the level of the top of the pork. Cook over high heat until the liquid comes to a simmer, cover tightly with a lid or aluminum foil, and transfer to the bottom rack of the oven.

4. Braise the pork for 1½ to 2 hours, until meat is meltingly tender. To test, insert a knife or skewer into a thick section; there should be no resistance and the juices should run clear. Cool completely at room temperature and then refrigerate, covered, overnight.

PREPARATION FOR THE CREOLE BAKED BEANS

1. Preheat oven to 300°.

2. In a heavy pot, cook the sausage in the olive oil over medium-low heat until it is well browned and crusty bits stick to the pot. Add the onion, celery, and peppers and cook until softened and lightly caramelized.

3. Add the garlic, bay leaf, red pepper flakes, and Creole spice and cook 2 minutes. Stir in the sugar, mustard, and tomatoes, then add the neckbones or hock, drained red beans, and enough chicken stock to cover by 1½ inches. Stir well, bring to a boil, and cover with a round of baker's parchment or aluminum foil, then a tight-fitting lid. Transfer to the oven and bake for 1½ hours; check the stock regularly and add more if necessary. Cook until the beans are tender and most of the stock is absorbed. Season generously. Remove the neck bones or hock and cut off the meat. Chop the meat and return it to the beans. Cool, then refrigerate overnight, or longer. As with all dried legumes, the flavor improves if these beans are made 1 to 2 days in advance.

ASSEMBLY

1. Remove the pork from the refrigerator; scrape all the congealed fat from the surface and warm the pan over medium-low heat for 10 minutes. Lift the pork

from the pan to a platter, strain the solids from the braising liquid, and return all but 1 1/2 cups of the braising liquid to the roasting pan. Return the pork to the pan and warm over medium heat to heat the pork thoroughly. Keep warm.

2. Transfer the reserved braising liquid to a saucepan, bring to a boil, and cook over medium heat, skimming impurities, until reduced by half. Season and keep warm.

3. Heat the beans in a saucepot until warmed through. Season, add the oregano and parsley, adjust the acidity with cider vinegar, and divide between 6 warm bowls. With a slotted spoon, lift the hot pork osso buco from the braising liquid and place one in each bowl.

4. In a small bowl, toss the red mustard with the corn relish, olive oil, salt, and black pepper. Spoon reduced braising liquid over the pork and divide the salad on top of each portion. Serve immediately, with rice on the side.

Note: Order pork osso buco from your butcher, 1 1/2–2 inches thick, approximately 16 ounces each, skin removed.

Herb-Crusted Rack of Pork on Brunswick "Stew"

SERVES 8

In these times of pork bred to be leaner, this extremely flavorful crust seals in moisture and forms a crunchy counterpoint to the juicy roast. (Note: Wonderful, voluptuous pork from Niman Ranch is available from D'Artagnan [see Sources].) We have found that the crust adheres better after cooking if you coat the roast well in advance and refrigerate it. Just be sure to remove it from the refrigerator at least 30 to 60 minutes before roasting.

The Brunswick "stew" forms a chunky vegetable sauce for the roast. We like to serve this accompanied by one of our spoonbread variations (page 168).

INGREDIENTS FOR THE PORK

1 8-rib center-cut pork rack, blade bone and chine removed, rib bones frenched
1 cup dried bread crumbs
1/2 cup roasted garlic purée (page 245)
2 tablespoons chopped parsley
2 tablespoons chopped rosemary
2 tablespoons chopped sage
1 1/2 teaspoons salt
1 teaspoon black pepper, ground
1/2 cup olive oil
8 rosemary sprigs for garnish (optional)

PREPARATION

1. Combine the bread crumbs, roasted garlic purée, herbs, salt, pepper, and olive oil. Coat the surface of the pork with this mixture and place on a rack in a roasting pan. This may be done ahead of time, in which case the pork should be removed from refrigeration for 30 to 60 minutes prior to roasting.

2. Preheat oven to 350°. Roast the pork in the middle of the oven for 35 to 45 minutes, or until it reaches 145° internal temperature or desired doneness. Let rest for 15 minutes.

INGREDIENTS FOR THE BRUNSWICK "STEW"

¼ cup rendered duck fat, or peanut oil

4 ounces sweet onion, finely diced

2 ounces carrot, finely diced

3 ounces celery, finely diced

3 ounces green bell pepper, finely diced

2 tablespoons garlic, minced

½ teaspoon crushed red pepper flakes

1 bay leaf

1 pound fresh baby butterbeans or limas (or frozen limas)

2 cups chicken stock

4 ears Silver Queen or Summersweet white corn,
    husked, silked, and cut from the cob

4 ounces Red Bliss or Yukon Gold potatoes, scrubbed and cut into ¼-inch dice,
    then poached in salted water until tender and reserved

1 cup fresh tomato concassé (page 237), combined with 1 tablespoon each
    chopped rosemary and sage, 2 tablespoons cider vinegar, and 2 tablespoons
    peanut or olive oil

2 tablespoons unsalted butter

salt and black pepper to taste

PREPARATION

1. In a nonreactive pan, over medium heat, cook the onion, carrot, celery, and green pepper in the duck fat until softened but not colored. Add the garlic, red pepper flakes, and bay leaf and cook 1 minute.

2. Add the baby butterbeans and chicken stock, bring to a boil, reduce to a simmer, and cook until the beans are tender. Stir in the corn and cook 3 minutes. (May be prepared ahead up to this point.)

3. Heat the butterbeans and corn over medium heat. Stir in the potatoes and warm through. Add the tomato-herb mixture and then stir in the butter; season with salt and pepper and keep warm.

ASSEMBLY AND PRESENTATION

Divide the Brunswick "stew" onto plates. If serving with spoonbread, place spoonbread beside the "stew" on each plate. Slicing between the ribs, slice the pork into chops and place a chop on each plate, atop the bed of "stew," with the bone resting on the spoonbread, if included. Garnish with a rosemary sprig if desired.

Beef Shortribs in Barbecued Onion Sauce with Grilled Spring Leeks & Roasted Garlic Grits

SERVES 8

Our friend David Auerbach is the king of "brown food." If there is a braised dish on the menu when he comes in, we know he'll order it, because braised dishes ultimately have the most soul. Depth of flavor derived from careful searing and languid cooking in a flavorful liquid is innately satisfying and defines "comfort food" for us. This dish requires advance preparation and is all the better for it.

INGREDIENTS FOR THE SHORTRIBS

8–10 pounds beef shortribs, cut crosswise

1 bottle decent, but not great, Zinfandel or other hearty red wine

2 onions, peeled and sliced

3 carrots, peeled and sliced

3 ribs celery, sliced

3 bay leaves

12 cloves garlic, crushed

1 tablespoon black peppercorns

6 sprigs fresh thyme

6 sprigs fresh rosemary

salt and black pepper

INGREDIENTS FOR THE SAUCE

olive oil

6 ounces onion, ideally Vidalias, diced fine

¼ cup garlic cloves, sliced

2 bay leaves

2 jalapeños, seeded and minced

1 poblano chile, seeded and chopped

1 large red bell pepper, seeded and chopped

1 teaspoon cayenne pepper

2 tablespoons chile powder

1 teaspoon tomato paste

1 tablespoon dried oregano

¼ cup red wine vinegar

2 tablespoons tamarind concentrate (available at Oriental markets)

1 teaspoon anchovy paste (or finely chopped anchovies)

2 cups Zinfandel

1 cup chopped canned tomatoes, with juice reserved

1 cup juice from tomatoes

salt, black pepper, and Worcestershire sauce to taste

16 baby spring leeks, tops and roots trimmed, washed

1 recipe creamy roasted garlic grits (page 159)

8 rosemary sprigs

PREPARATION FOR THE SHORTRIBS (BEGIN 2 DAYS AHEAD)

1. Combine all of the ingredients except the shortribs to make a marinade. Add the shortribs and toss to coat. Refrigerate, turning in the marinade occasionally, for 24 hours. Remove from refrigeration 1 hour before cooking and wipe off the marinade, reserving the liquid and vegetables. Light the grill, if using to sear shortribs. Preheat oven to 300°.

2. Season the shortribs generously with salt and pepper. Sear over medium-hot coals, turning until well caramelized. (You can also sear in batches in olive oil in a large sauté pan.) Transfer the shortribs to a nonreactive roasting pan large enough to hold them in one layer.

3. Strain the marinade over the shortribs; remove the herbs from the vegetables and scatter them over the meat. In olive oil, sauté the vegetables until lightly browned and then scatter them over the shortribs. Add water to the roasting pan to come three-quarters of the way up the sides of the shortribs; place the roasting pan on the range and heat over medium-high heat until just simmering. Seal with aluminum foil and braise in the oven 1 ½ to 2 hours, until very tender and the bones are loose. Cool at room temperature and then refrigerate overnight.

4. Remove from refrigeration and scrape the congealed fat from the surface of the braising liquid. Warm the roasting pan over low heat to liquify and remove the shortribs to a cutting board. Remove the bones from the shortribs and trim the gristle and elastin casing from the bone sockets. Divide into one- and two-piece portions and transfer to a large, heavy saucepan. Strain the braising liquid over the shortribs and set aside.

1. Heat olive oil in a large nonreactive saucepan; add the onions and cook over medium heat until softened and lightly caramelized. Add the garlic, bay leaves, jalapeños, poblano chile, and red bell pepper; cook, covered, over low heat until softened.

2. Add the cayenne, chile powder, tomato paste, and oregano. Cook 1 minute and then add all the remaining ingredients. Bring to a simmer and cook 30 minutes. Remove the bay leaves, purée in a food processor, and pass through the fine blade of a food mill. Cool and refrigerate.

ASSEMBLY

1. Blanch the baby leeks in boiling salted water until tender. Cool in ice water and drain thoroughly. Toss the leeks in olive oil and season, then grill or roast in a 350° oven until hot, about 10 minutes. Set aside in a warm place.

2. Heat the shortribs in the braising liquid over medium-low heat until warmed through. Warm the barbecued onion sauce over medium heat.

3. Divide the creamy grits between 8 warm, shallow bowls or platters. Place a portion of shortribs on top of the grits in each bowl. Bring the braising liquid to a boil and add 1 cup of the braising liquid to the sauce until the consistency is smooth; adjust the seasoning. Ladle onion sauce over and around the shortribs and garnish each portion with 2 leeks twisted together on top. Stick a rosemary sprig into each portion and serve immediately.

Grilled Beef Tenderloin in Cabernet Sauce with Roquefort & Summer Vegetable Chopped Salad

SERVES 6

Steaks and blue cheese are so easy to match that we wanted to juxtapose them in a different fashion. While we generally prefer a ribeye or strip steak for our steak dinners, tenderloin, with its sumptuous texture, is the right choice against the crunchy vegetables, Roquefort, and bacon in this dish. Serve with duck fat potatoes (page 110) if you want a starch accompaniment.

INGREDIENTS FOR THE BEEF

6 beef filet mignons (approximately 7 ounces each), trimmed
2 tablespoons balsamic vinegar
2 cloves garlic, crushed
4 sprigs rosemary, bruised
¼ cup olive oil
1 teaspoon coarsely cracked black peppercorns
salt

PREPARATION

Coat the steaks with a marinade combining all the other ingredients except the salt. Refrigerate 3 to 4 hours or overnight. Remove from refrigeration 1 hour before cooking and wipe excess marinade off the steaks.

INGREDIENTS FOR THE SAUCE

1 cup onion, chopped into 1-inch pieces

½ cup carrot, chopped into 1-inch pieces

½ cup celery, chopped into 1-inch pieces

¼ cup olive oil

6 cloves garlic, crushed

2 bay leaves

2 tablespoons tomato paste

¼ cup balsamic vinegar

¼ cup red wine vinegar

2 cups red wine, preferably Cabernet

1½ quarts veal stock (page 230) or roasted chicken stock (page 228)

salt and black pepper to taste

PREPARATION

1. In a heavy-bottomed pot, cook the onions, carrots, and celery in olive oil over medium heat until well browned. Add the garlic, bay leaves, and tomato paste; cook 1 minute, stirring. Add the vinegars and wine, bring to a boil, and simmer until reduced by two-thirds. Add the veal or chicken stock, bring to a boil, and simmer, skimming occasionally, until reduced by two-thirds. Strain through a fine-mesh strainer. Cool and refrigerate if not using immediately.

2. Return the sauce to the heat and simmer until it lightly coats the back of a spoon. Season with salt and pepper and keep warm.

INGREDIENTS FOR THE CHOPPED SALAD

¼ cup zucchini (use only the green outside part), cut into small dice

¼ cup gold zucchini or yellow squash (outside part only), cut into small dice

¼ cup green beans, cut into ¼-inch rounds

¼ cup yellow wax beans, cut into ¼-inch rounds

¼ cup red onion, cut into small dice and tossed in 1 teaspoon red wine vinegar

¼ cup tomato concassé (page 237)

¼ cup roasted red bell pepper, cut into small dice

1 cup frisée lettuce or mizzuna, washed and torn in small pieces

1 tablespoon fresh mint, chopped

2 teaspoons fresh rosemary, chopped

1 tablespoon flat-leaf parsley, chopped

½ cup Roquefort cheese, crumbled

½ cup crisp bacon, crumbled

salt and black pepper to taste

PREPARATION

Cut up all the vegetables, keeping them separate. In boiling salted water,
separately blanch the zucchini, yellow squash, green beans, and wax beans for
10 to 30 seconds to set their color, then immediately plunge them into ice water
to stop the cooking. Drain each thoroughly and reserve. (The red onions are
tossed in vinegar, as indicated above, and the tomato and roasted pepper undergo
no further cooking.)

INGREDIENTS FOR THE DRESSING

    1 egg yolk
    2 tablespoons red wine vinegar
    2 teaspoons Dijon mustard
    1 teaspoon minced garlic
    ¼ cup Roquefort cheese, crumbled
    ¼ cup safflower oil
    ¼ cup buttermilk (you may substitute sour cream)
    salt and black pepper to taste

PREPARATION

In a blender or small food processor, combine the egg yolk, vinegar, mustard,
garlic, and Roquefort. Pulse to blend. With the machine running, drizzle in the
safflower oil and then the buttermilk. Season with salt and pepper and reserve.

INGREDIENT FOR THE GARNISH

    2 tablespoons chive batons, cut 1 inch in length

ASSEMBLY AND PRESENTATION

    1. Light the grill and let the coals cook down to a medium-hot fire. Season
       the steaks liberally with salt and grill to the desired degree of doneness, about
       4 minutes on each side for medium rare. Remove to a rack and keep warm.
    2. Combine the vegetables for the chopped salad in a bowl; add the frisée, herbs,
       Roquefort, bacon, and a little salt and coarsely ground pepper. Spoon the
       dressing over the vegetables and toss until well coated; check the seasoning.
    3. Divide the salad between 6 warm plates, placing a steak on top of the salad on
       each plate. Pour any juices from the steaks into the sauce and spoon the sauce
       over and around the steaks. Sprinkle with chive batons and serve immediately.

Grilled Lamb Chops with a Ragout of Baby Artichokes, Olives, & Oven-Dried Tomatoes

SERVES 4

This dish is carefully calculated to appeal to lamb lovers, mashed potato lovers, artichoke lovers, and, most important, garlic lovers. The aioli marinade for the chops coats them and gives them a wonderful crust; the buttermilk mashed new potatoes, with which we customarily serve this, contrast fabulously with the artichoke ragout for a wonderful balance of flavors. Vampires beware!

INGREDIENTS FOR THE LAMB

    8 lamb loin chops (5 ounces each), closely trimmed

    1 egg yolk

    2 tablespoons white wine

    2 tablespoons roasted garlic purée (page 245)

    ½ cup olive oil

    1½ tablespoons chopped rosemary

    salt and black pepper to taste

INGREDIENTS FOR THE ARTICHOKES

    2 pounds baby artichokes

    ½ cup olive oil

    ½ cup onion, finely diced

    ½ cup carrot, peeled and finely diced

    2 ribs celery, finely diced

    2 bay leaves

    ¼ cup chopped garlic

    ½ teaspoon crushed red pepper flakes

    ¼ cup lemon juice

    ½ cup white wine

    1 cup chicken stock + additional stock if needed

    salt and black pepper to taste

    ½ cup chopped oven-dried tomatoes (page 237)

    ½ cup pitted calamata olives, chopped

    ¼ cup fresh thyme or lemon thyme leaves

    1 tablespoon rosemary leaves, minced

    2 tablespoons flat-leaf parsley, chopped

INGREDIENTS FOR THE GREMOLATA GARNISH

    1 teaspoon freshly minced garlic

    1 teaspoon minced lemon zest

    1 teaspoon chopped parsley

    1 teaspoon chopped rosemary

OPTIONAL INGREDIENT FOR SERVING

    1 recipe buttermilk mashed new potatoes (page 161)

1. Prepare the lamb. In a bowl, whisk together the egg yolk, wine, and roasted garlic purée until smooth. Slowly drizzle in olive oil, whisking to form an emulsion. Thin with a little more wine if necessary; the mixture should have the consistency of a loose mayonnaise. Fold in the chopped rosemary and coat the chops with the mayonnaise. Refrigerate for 3 to 4 hours, or overnight; return to room temperature before cooking.

2. Prepare the artichokes. Trim the stem end of each artichoke and peel the leaves until the pale yellow interior leaves are exposed. Cut the spiny tip off, pare the base with a small knife, and put the artichokes in a bowl of water acidulated with the juice of 1 lemon.

3. Cook the artichokes. Heat the olive oil in a heavy-bottomed pan over medium heat. Add the onions, carrots, and celery and cook until the vegetables are softened. Add the bay leaves, garlic, and red pepper flakes; cook 1 minute. Add the lemon juice, wine, and stock and bring to a simmer. Drain the artichokes, add them to the broth, and simmer until the artichokes are tender at the base. Season with salt and pepper. Cool.

4. Prepare the buttermilk mashed new potatoes, if you are serving them, and keep warm. Prepare the gremolata by combining all of the ingredients. Light the grill and let the coals burn down to a medium-hot fire. Remove the chops from the marinade but do not wipe off excess marinade. Season with salt and pepper. Grill the chops, about 3 minutes on each side for medium rare. Remove and keep warm.

5. Assembly. Heat the artichokes over medium heat until hot. Stir in the oven-dried tomatoes and olives; check the seasoning. Stir in the herbs. Divide the mashed potatoes between hot plates, mounding in the center. Place 2 chops on each plate on top of the potatoes and spoon artichoke ragout around. Sprinkle the chops with gremolata and serve immediately.

Venison Medallions in Zinfandel–Black Pepper Jus

SERVES 4

If you hunt, know a hunter, or happen to be friends with a lettuce farmer who can't afford deer in his garden, you may be fortunate enough to have wild venison for this dish. The marinade is intended to enhance milder farm-raised venison, which is available from your butcher or a specialty meat supplier (see Sources). It will not detract from wild deer, but you may not wish to marinate the meat as long as we indicate, lest you lose that wonderful wild taste.

We recommend serving venison rare if it's from the loin, as it is meltingly tender and most flavorful that way. If you prefer your meat more cooked, increase the cooking time but be careful not to overcook: venison is quite lean and will dry out in no time. We serve these medallions with garlicky sautéed broccoli rabe and a sweet potato and leek gratin (page 163).

INGREDIENTS FOR THE VENISON AND MARINADE

1½ pounds boneless venison loin, silverskin removed and trimmed,
   with trimmings reserved

1 teaspoon fennel seed

1 teaspoon coriander seed

1 tablespoon black peppercorns

8 juniper berries

4 cloves garlic, sliced

2 shallots, sliced

6 sprigs fresh thyme

2–3 bay leaves

zest of 1 orange, grated

1½ cups red wine

¼ cup olive oil + olive oil for sautéing medallions

salt and freshly ground black pepper

INGREDIENTS FOR THE JUS

reserved venison trimmings

2 tablespoons olive oil

1 cup onion, cut into medium dice

2 carrots, cut into medium dice

2 ribs celery, cut into medium dice

½ teaspoon fennel seed, cracked

1 teaspoon coriander seed, cracked

3–4 juniper berries

8 cloves garlic, sliced

2 bay leaves

½ cup preserved black currants in syrup (see note)

¼ cup red wine vinegar

2 cups Zinfandel or fruity red wine

1 quart venison stock (you may substitute veal stock [page 230]
   or roasted chicken stock [page 228])

2 tablespoons red wine garlic purée (page 246)

1 large sprig fresh thyme

1 teaspoon coarsely cracked black peppercorns

2 tablespoons unsalted butter

salt to taste

INGREDIENTS FOR THE GARNISH

4 thyme sprigs

1 teaspoon finely ground black pepper

PREPARATION FOR THE VENISON

1. In a dry pan over medium-high heat, toast the fennel seed, coriander seed, and
black peppercorns until fragrant. Cool and coarsely grind in a spice mill or with
a mortar and pestle. Add the juniper berries to the pan and roll them around

over medium heat until shiny. Remove the berries and mash them with the side of a knife.

2. Combine the garlic, shallots, spices, herbs, and orange zest in a shallow nonreactive pan large enough to hold the venison loin in one layer. Add the red wine and olive oil; roll the loin in the marinade and refrigerate overnight, turning occasionally.

3. Remove the meat from the marinade, wipe off excess, and cut the loin into 8 equal portions. Reserve at room temperature.

PREPARATION FOR THE JUS

1. Brown the trimmings from the venison loin in olive oil until deeply caramelized. Remove and reserve.

2. In the olive oil, brown the onions, carrots, and celery over medium heat until caramelized and deeply colored. Add the fennel seed, coriander seed, juniper berries, garlic, and bay leaves and cook 1 to 2 minutes.

3. Add the currants and their juice and the red wine vinegar; mash the currants against the bottom of the pan. Add the Zinfandel and browned trimmings and bring to a simmer, reducing by two-thirds. Add the stock, bring to a simmer, and reduce, skimming occasionally, by three-quarters. Stir in the red wine garlic purée, thyme, and cracked black pepper. Remove from heat, steep for 5 minutes to infuse, and strain into a small saucepan.

4. Warm the jus over medium heat, whisk in the butter, and season with salt and with additional black pepper if desired. Keep warm.

ASSEMBLY

1. Heat 1 or 2 large sauté pans over medium-high heat for 3 minutes. Dry the venison portions on both sides and season liberally with salt and freshly ground black pepper.

2. Film the pan(s) with olive oil and add the venison carefully to the hot oil. Do not crowd the pan(s): you want to sear the meat quickly and not steam it. Cook the medallions for 1 minute on the first side, then turn and cook 1 minute longer for rare, or a bit longer if you desire your meat more done. Remove the medallions from the pan(s) and keep warm.

3. Divide the broccoli rabe and sweet potato and leek gratin, if you are serving them, between 4 hot plates. Place 2 medallions on each plate and spoon some of the jus over and around each. Garnish with a thyme sprig and sprinkle a little finely ground black pepper around the plate. Serve immediately.

Note: Preserved black currants in syrup are available at specialty food shops. You may omit them or use fresh red or black currants if they're available.

Rabbit Confit with Marinated Baby Artichokes, Newly Dug Potatoes, & Spring Vegetables

SERVES 4

This dish is a gorgeous plate to celebrate the vegetables of spring. It is inspired by the cooking of our friend Frank Stitt, the chef at Highlands Bar & Grill in Birmingham, Alabama. Rabbit treated in this fashion is both meaty and delicate at the same time and is perfectly offset by the earthy young root vegetables, faintly sweet artichokes, and crunchy peas. (If tender pea tendrils are available, by all means substitute them for the spinach.) The lemony herb broth links all the flavors without overwhelming any of them.

Fresh rabbit legs may be ordered from your specialty butcher or are available by mail order (see Sources).

INGREDIENTS FOR THE RABBIT

    4 young fryer rabbit legs, hip bone removed (about 1 ¾ pounds)
    2 teaspoons salt
    1 teaspoon medium-grind black pepper
    1 teaspoon cracked fennel seeds
    1 tablespoon thyme leaves
    1 ½ tablespoons rosemary leaves, roughly chopped
    peel of 1 lemon, roughly chopped
    8 cloves garlic, peeled
    4 bay leaves
    olive oil as needed
    ½ cup dry vermouth
    ¼ cup chervil sprigs for garnish

INGREDIENTS FOR THE BROTH

    3 tablespoons olive oil (from rabbit confit)
    6 shallots, finely diced
    1 bay leaf
    ¼ cup lemon juice
    2 tablespoons tarragon vinegar
    1 cup dry vermouth
    1 cup white wine
    1 ½ cups rabbit stock or roasted chicken stock (page 228)
    2 tablespoons unsalted butter
    2 tablespoons combined tarragon and chervil, chopped
    salt and black pepper to taste

INGREDIENTS FOR THE VEGETABLES

    ½ pound tiny new red or gold potatoes,
        ideally the size of a quarter or smaller, washed
    2 sprigs fresh thyme
    2 bay leaves

4 cloves garlic

⅓ cup olive oil (from rabbit confit)

8 small baby carrots, steamed until tender, peeled, and split lengthwise

4 small white turnips, steamed until tender, peeled, and cut into sixths

4 small gold or Chioggia beets, steamed until tender, peeled, and cut into sixths

½ cup blanched English peas (or substitute 1 cup blanched tiny sugarsnap peas)

1 cup marinated baby artichokes (page 247)

1 cup young spinach leaves, stemmed and washed

1 tablespoon fresh chervil leaves

1 tablespoon thyme leaves

1 tablespoon chives, cut ½ inch in length

1 tablespoon mint leaves, cut into chiffonade

salt and black pepper to taste

PREPARATION FOR THE RABBIT

1. Begin the preparation 2 days in advance. Pat the rabbit legs dry and rub them with salt, pepper, fennel seed, thyme, rosemary, and lemon peel. Refrigerate overnight, or for 12 hours.

2. Preheat oven to 300°. Combine the rabbit legs with the garlic cloves and bay leaves in an ovenproof casserole. Add olive oil to cover. Heat over medium heat to 180° (use an instant-read or deep-frying thermometer), cover tightly with foil, and cook in the oven for 30 to 35 minutes, or until tender. Cool completely and refrigerate overnight. (May be prepared 3 or 4 days in advance.)

PREPARATION FOR THE BROTH

Take 3 tablespoons of olive oil from the rabbit confit and heat it in a saucepan over medium heat. Add the shallots and bay leaf, reduce the heat, and stew until the shallots are softened. Add the lemon juice, vinegar, vermouth, and white wine, bring to a simmer, and cook until reduced by three-quarters. Add the stock and cook gently until reduced by a third. Remove from heat, strain, and reserve. Refrigerate if not using immediately.

PREPARATION FOR THE VEGETABLES

1. Preheat oven to 350°. Toss the new potatoes with the sprigs of thyme, bay leaves, whole garlic cloves, and ⅓ cup of olive oil from the rabbit confit. Season generously with salt and pepper, transfer to an ovenproof casserole, and roast until tender, about 25 minutes. Remove the garlic, thyme, and bay leaves and discard. Reserve the potatoes.

2. Steam the carrots, turnips, and beets separately until tender. Transfer to a bowl of ice water as they're done to arrest the cooking, then drain, peel, and cut as directed. Reserve.

3. Peel and blanch the peas (or sugarsnaps). Reserve.

4. Cut the marinated artichokes into quarters and reserve.

ASSEMBLY

1. Remove the rabbit legs from refrigeration and lift from the oil, wiping off any herbs or lemon peel that may be clinging to them. Preheat oven to 350° and

heat a large ovenproof skillet over medium heat. Film the skillet with some olive oil from the confit and brown the legs on all sides. Add ½ cup vermouth, cover the skillet, and transfer to the oven for 10 to 15 minutes, until the legs are warmed through.

2. Heat a large skillet over medium heat. Add 2 tablespoons of oil from the confit to the pan and add the roasted potatoes. Cook until warmed through. Add the turnips, carrots, and beets and warm 2 to 3 minutes. Add the artichokes and toss to combine. Add the peas and spinach; toss once or twice just to wilt the spinach. Add the herbs and season to taste. Divide the vegetables between 4 warm, shallow bowls.

3. Heat the broth over medium-high heat until hot. Off the heat, whisk in the butter, then add the herbs and season to taste. Place a rabbit leg next to the vegetables in each bowl and spoon some broth over and around the leg and vegetables. Garnish the legs with chervil and serve immediately.

Gabriel's Favorite Crispy Parmesan Chicken with Lemon & Capers

SERVES 4

This recipe is dedicated to our son Gabriel, who at the age of five proclaimed capers to be his favorite green vegetable. This dish appears with regularity when a fast and easy dinner is needed in the Barker household, and a classic variation using veal sweetbreads (sans Parmesan cheese) is occasionally featured at the Grill. This preparation works equally well with turkey, veal, or pork cutlets.

Gabriel's favorite accompaniment is a garlicky sauté of broccoli florets or asparagus tossed with a little Dijon mustard.

INGREDIENTS FOR THE CHICKEN

4 (6-ounce) boneless, skinless chicken breasts, trimmed and lightly pounded

½ cup flour

2 eggs

¾ cup plain dry bread crumbs

¼ cup finely grated Parmesan cheese

1 tablespoon chopped parsley

salt and freshly ground black pepper

3 tablespoons olive oil

INGREDIENTS FOR THE LEMON-CAPER BROWN BUTTER

4 tablespoons unsalted butter

2 tablespoons capers

2 tablespoons lemon juice

1 tablespoon chopped parsley

salt and black pepper to taste

PREPARATION FOR THE CHICKEN

1. Place the flour in a shallow bowl or pie plate. Beat the eggs in another shallow bowl or pie plate. Combine the bread crumbs with the Parmesan cheese and parsley in a third bowl or pie plate. Season the crumbs to taste with salt and pepper.
2. Dredge each chicken breast in flour, shaking off any excess. Dip into the beaten egg and then coat evenly with the bread crumb mixture. When all are coated, refrigerate on a plate for 20 to 30 minutes.
3. Preheat oven to 250°.
4. Heat the olive oil in a large nonstick sauté pan over medium heat. Add the chicken and cook until crisp and golden brown (approximately 4 to 5 minutes). Turn and repeat on the other side. Remove the chicken to a warm plate and keep in a low-temperature oven while you prepare the sauce.

PREPARATION FOR THE LEMON-CAPER BROWN BUTTER

Place the butter in a small skillet. Over medium-high heat, cook until the butter begins to lightly brown and smells nutty. Add the capers and fry them for 30 seconds. Add the lemon juice, parsley, and salt and pepper to taste. Remove from heat. Divide the chicken breasts between warm plates and spoon sauce over each. Serve immediately.

Simple Roast Chicken with Duck Fat Potatoes

SERVES 2 TO 3

On our nights off, we have probably prepared this dinner more than any other over the years. Quick, delicious, satisfying to all the senses, and a perfect justification for opening a bottle of red wine—what more do you need? Maybe a small salad on the side and nothing more.

INGREDIENTS FOR THE CHICKEN

> 1 3½-pound whole fryer
> salt and freshly ground black pepper
> 1 lemon
> 1 bay leaf, preferably fresh
> a handful of herbs of your choice

INGREDIENTS FOR THE POTATOES

> 1 pound Idaho or large Yukon Gold potatoes
> salt
> rendered duck fat (see Sources), or peanut or olive oil

PREPARATION FOR THE CHICKEN

1. Preheat oven to 375°.
2. Wash the chicken, inside and out, and dry thoroughly. Season the cavity liberally with salt and pepper. Prick a lemon with a skewer or toothpick a few times and shove it into the cavity with the bay leaf and herbs. Secure the skin over the cavity's opening with a toothpick or a metal skewer. Loosely tie the legs together and season the bird generously on the exterior with salt and pepper.
3. Place the bird breast-side down in a small roasting pan. Roast for 20 minutes, then turn the chicken breast-side up and roast for 20 minutes longer. Raise the oven temperature to 425° and roast for 20 minutes. The chicken should be crispy and golden; the juices at the leg joint should run clear.
4. Rest the chicken for at least 5 to 10 minutes before carving. Remove the chicken to a cutting board, pour off the fat from the roasting pan, and deglaze the pan with a little wine, stock, or water if you desire some pan juices.
5. Cut the chicken into serving pieces and divide between warm plates. Spoon a little of the pan juices over the chicken and accompany with roasted potatoes. Serve immediately.

PREPARATION FOR THE POTATOES

1. Peel the potatoes and cut into ¾- to 1-inch cubes. Cover with cold water in a saucepot, season with salt, and bring to a boil. Blanch until tender yet firm; drain and dry thoroughly.
2. Heat duck fat to a depth of ⅓ inch in a skillet over medium-high heat. Add the potatoes in one layer, reduce the heat to medium, and cook, turning, until deeply golden crisp on all sides, about 6 to 8 minutes. Remove from the pan to drain on paper toweling; season with salt and serve immediately.

Grilled Quail on Crawfish Jambalaya Risotto with Smoked Tomato & Sage Essence

SERVES 8 AS AN APPETIZER OR 4 AS AN ENTRÉE

Quail are as close as we come to wild birds on our regular menu at the restaurant. Their delicate gaminess lends itself to numerous flavor combinations. They make an excellent and substantial first course, or a satisfying dinner, with the crawfish jambalaya risotto, a not so subtle nod to the field and stream association. We love quail grilled and often incorporate a little sweetness into the marinade we use for them so they can caramelize and crisp as they cook. Be sure to encourage your guests to pick the legs up with their fingers, offering finger bowls afterward.

INGREDIENTS FOR THE QUAIL

> 8 semiboneless fresh quail (4–5 ounces each) or frozen quail,
> > defrosted for 24 hours in the refrigerator
> 1 tablespoon sorghum or unsulfured molasses
> 2 tablespoons bourbon
> 2 shallots, peeled and sliced thin
> 1 tablespoon fresh sage leaves, coarsely chopped
> 1 teaspoon coarsely ground black pepper
> 2 ounces peanut oil

PREPARATION

1. Trim the wing tips from the quail and reserve. Make an incision in the skin at the base of the breast bone and insert the legs through the incision.
2. Stir the molasses and bourbon together and add the remaining ingredients to make the marinade.
3. Coat the quail with the marinade and refrigerate, turning occasionally, for 4 hours, or overnight. Remove the quail from the marinade 30 minutes prior to cooking.
4. Light the grill. Season the quail with salt and grill them over a medium-hot fire, breast-side down, for 2 minutes. Turn and cook 2 minutes longer or until the leg meat feels firm. Remove and keep warm.

INGREDIENTS FOR THE SMOKED TOMATO AND SAGE ESSENCE

> reserved quail wing tips
> 2 tablespoons peanut oil
> 4 shallots, minced
> 2 tablespoons garlic, minced
> 1 bay leaf
> 1 tablespoon sorghum or unsulfured molasses
> ¼ cup bourbon
> 2 tablespoons cider vinegar
> 2 tablespoons red wine vinegar
> 1 cup red wine

1 quart roasted chicken stock (page 228) or light chicken stock

½ cup smoked tomato purée (page 238)

2 tablespoons roasted garlic purée (page 245)

2 tablespoons coarsely chopped sage

salt and black pepper to taste

PREPARATION

1. In a 2-quart saucepan, heat the oil over medium heat. Brown the quail bones, stirring for 10 minutes until nicely colored. Add the shallots, garlic, and bay leaf; cook 2 to 3 minutes, until softened and aromatic. Add the molasses, bourbon, cider vinegar, and red wine vinegar; bring to a boil and reduce by three-quarters, to a syrupy consistency. Add the red wine and reduce by three-quarters. Add the stock, bring to a boil, and simmer, skimming any impurities, for 20 minutes, until reduced by half. Strain into a 1-quart saucepan; cool and reserve.

2. Heat the sauce to a boil and reduce to 1 cup. Stir in the smoked tomato purée, roasted garlic purée, and sage and steep for 10 minutes. Season, strain, and keep warm.

INGREDIENTS FOR THE GARNISH AND ASSEMBLY

½ cup scallion greens, cut thin on the bias

½ cup tomato concassé (page 237), marinated with 1 teaspoon cider vinegar and a grinding of black pepper

8 sprigs fresh sage

crawfish jambalaya risotto (page 165)

smoked tomato and sage essence (see recipe above)

ASSEMBLY

1. Finish the risotto as described in step 3 of the recipe (page 166).

2. Divide the risotto between 8 large, warm, shallow bowls. Top the risotto with a quail and spoon the smoked tomato and sage essence over and around the quail. Scatter scallions and marinated tomato concassé over all and garnish with a sage sprig.

Our Thanksgiving Turkey with "140" Cloves of Garlic

SERVES 14 OF OUR FAMILY AND FRIENDS

Our Thanksgiving turkey is, first and foremost, inspired by Karen's Aunt Dora, who was always responsible for her family's annual bird. The centerpiece of a multicourse, vastly complicated gourmet feast prepared by Iris, Karen's cousin and Dora's daughter, the turkey came to the table redolent of garlic and pristine in its simple glory.

Credit, of course, is also due James Beard, who inspired countless converts with his classic interpretation of "chicken with 40 cloves of garlic." The confit fat basting is Ben's contribution and yields a gloriously deep mahogany skin and fantastic flavor.

Numerous sources are available for organic, hormone-free turkeys, which are vastly superior in every way. Exercise caution, however, as they cook much faster than com-

mercially injected birds, and while the overcooked turkey may be traditional, it is a reve-
lation to eat a juicy, moist Thanksgiving fowl.

Serve with all the side dishes traditional to your family, or consider our Southern
greens (page 149), buttermilk mashed new potatoes (page 161), and wild mushroom
bread pudding (page 166).

INGREDIENTS FOR THE TURKEY

    1 21- to 25-pound fresh turkey, preferably a free-range organic bird
    4 large sprigs fresh sage
    6 large sprigs fresh thyme
    6–8 fresh bay leaves
    as many peeled garlic cloves as you can stuff into the turkey
    2 cups cold rendered duck fat—or better, fat from duck confit (page 118)
    salt and black pepper

INGREDIENTS FOR THE "GRAVY"

    2 tablespoons duck fat or peanut oil
    ½ onion, sliced thin
    2 bay leaves
    ½ cup sherry vinegar
    1½ cups Madeira
    1½ quarts roasted chicken stock (page 228)
    roasted garlic cloves (from the turkey)
    1 tablespoon fresh sage leaves, chopped
    1 tablespoon fresh thyme leaves, chopped
    salt and black pepper to taste

PREPARATION FOR THE TURKEY

1. The day before, remove the turkey from its plastic wrapper. Remove the giblets
   and neck and set them aside. Wash the turkey inside and out; dry thoroughly
   and put it in the refrigerator overnight to dry out the skin and cavity. Remove
   the turkey from the refrigerator at least 1 hour before cooking.
2. Preheat oven to 350°. Season the interior cavity and neck cavity liberally with
   salt and freshly ground black pepper. Divide the sage, thyme, and bay leaves
   between the body cavity and neck cavity. Shove as many cloves of peeled garlic
   into each cavity as possible; secure the neck skin with a skewer or toothpick and
   reposition the legs or tie them with butcher's twine.
3. Using your hands, slather duck fat on all the exposed skin of the turkey until
   well coated. Season liberally with salt and pepper and position the bird in a
   roasting pan, breast-side down. Place the neck in the immediate proximity of its
   original location; reserve the remaining giblets for another use.
4. Roast the turkey, breast-side down, for 45 minutes on the bottom rack of the
   oven. Remove from the oven and, with an assistant, turn the bird breast-side up.
   Using a pastry brush, baste all surfaces of the bird with melted duck fat from
   the roasting pan.

5. Return the turkey to the oven and roast for 10 minutes per pound, basting thoroughly every 20–30 minutes with the duck fat renderings in the roasting pan. Be careful not to overcook; test doneness by inserting a skewer into the inner thigh muscle; juices should be barely pinkish and the flesh still moist.

6. Remove the turkey to a cutting board to rest for at least 20 minutes, preferably 30. Extract the garlic cloves from the cavity and complete the gravy. Pour off all fat from the roasting pan; set the neck on a plate to snack on while finishing the gravy. (The neck will be meltingly tender and thoroughly infused with the duck fat flavor; it is the cook's prize, but be generous and insist that everyone taste "a little bit.") Deglaze the roasting pan with a little chicken stock so you can add the juices to the gravy.

7. Carve the turkey and transfer the meat to a platter.

PREPARATION FOR THE "GRAVY"

1. In a medium saucepan, heat the duck fat or peanut oil over medium heat. Add the onion and bay leaves; cook until the onion is soft and beginning to caramelize. Add the sherry vinegar and Madeira, bring to a simmer, and reduce by two-thirds.

2. Add the stock, bring to a simmer, and reduce by two-thirds, skimming. Strain into a clean saucepot and reserve until the turkey is finished roasting.

3. Add as many roasted garlic cloves as you like to the gravy and strain in the juices from the deglazed roasting pan. Warm over low heat, stir in the herbs, and season, adding a dash of sherry vinegar if necessary to bring into balance. Pass the gravy separately at table.

Pan-Roasted Duck Breast with Sun-Dried Cherry Conserve

SERVES 4

A simple pan roast of boneless duck breasts can be a fairly quick but elegant supper. We buy whole ducks, cut the breasts off, make a confit of the legs and gizzards, render the fat, and roast the bodies for stock so we get maximum utilization of the bird. Alternatively, you may order boneless fresh duck breasts from your butcher. The key to successful rendering of the duck breasts is in scoring the fat side of the breasts and searing them primarily on the skin side.

The cherry conserve may be prepared in advance. Sautéed Swiss chard and molasses mashed sweet potatoes (page 163) make appropriate accompaniments.

THE DUCK

4 fresh Muscovy or Peking duck breasts, boneless
(approximately 6–8 ounces each)

INGREDIENTS FOR THE MARINADE

1 tablespoon molasses (you may substitute pomegranate molasses)
1 tablespoon bourbon or brandy

2 cloves garlic, mashed with the side of a knife

2 shallots, peeled and sliced thin

1 teaspoon fresh thyme leaves

1 teaspoon cracked black peppercorns

2 tablespoons olive oil

INGREDIENTS FOR THE SUN-DRIED CHERRY CONSERVE

3 ounces sun-dried bing cherries

1 cup fruity red wine (e.g., Zinfandel or Dolcetto)

1 tablespoon olive oil

4 ounces sweet onion (Vidalia, Walla Walla, or Maui), peeled and sliced thin

1 tablespoon molasses or pomegranate molasses

1/4 cup balsamic vinegar

1 tablespoon fresh thyme leaves

pinch salt and freshly ground black pepper

INGREDIENTS FOR THE GARNISH

1/3 cup walnuts

1 tablespoon thyme leaves

PREPARATION

1. With a sharp knife, score the skin 1/8 inch deep on the duck breasts in a cross-hatch pattern without cutting through to the flesh. Combine the molasses, bourbon, garlic, and shallots and mix well. Add the thyme, black pepper, and olive oil and rub the marinade on the flesh side of the breasts, pressing the breasts together on the flesh side. Marinate 4 hours or overnight.

2. Make the conserve. Combine the cherries and wine in a nonreactive saucepan. Bring to a simmer, remove from the heat, and set aside. In a 1-quart saucepan, heat the olive oil over medium heat. Add the onions and cook, stirring occasionally, until softened and translucent but not browned. Add the molasses and balsamic vinegar and bring to a boil. Strain the cherry-soaking liquid into the mixture, bring back to a boil, and reduce by half. Stir in the cherries and thyme leaves and adjust the seasoning. Set aside. (The conserve may be prepared up to 2 days ahead.)

3. Toast the walnuts for 8 to 10 minutes in a 350° oven. Place in a tea towel and rub briskly to remove the skins. Set aside.

4. Remove the duck breasts from the refrigerator 30 minutes before cooking and wipe the marinade ingredients from the breasts. Season both sides with salt.

5. Warm the conserve over low heat; keep warm.

6. Heat a heavy steel or cast-iron pan over medium heat for 5 minutes. Add the breasts, skin-side down, and reduce the heat to medium-low. Render the fat in the skin for 5 to 8 minutes, until the skin is deeply bronzed and crisp. Turn and cook for 1 to 2 minutes on the flesh side for medium rare. Transfer to a cutting board and let rest for 5 minutes.

Slice the duck breasts thinly on the bias and arrange around mashed sweet potatoes, or whatever accompaniment you are using. Pour any duck juices from the cutting board into the cherry conserve and spoon the conserve around the duck breasts. Sprinkle with walnuts and thyme leaves. Serve immediately.

Duck Confit with Barbecued Lentils

SERVES 6

We have been making duck confit at the restaurant since our earliest days. It is the practical by-product of serving duck breasts as an entrée, wanting to render the fat for cooking purposes, and preserving the legs for later use in salads, soups, and rillettes or as first courses or entrées.

While the process may seem involved, having some confit on hand for a quick and satisfying supper, or when unexpected company arrives, is always a bonus. If your diet precludes the use of the amount of salt in the curing process, the salt quantity may be cut in half. In that instance, the legs should be used within 1 to 2 weeks.

You may also purchase prepared duck confit and rendered duck fat—D'Artagnan (see Sources) supplies excellent products—if you choose not to prepare your own.

INGREDIENTS FOR THE DUCK CURE

6 duck leg and thigh quarters, trimmed of excess fat
2½ tablespoons salt
2 tablespoons finely minced shallots
2 tablespoons chopped flat-leaf parsley
1 tablespoon black peppercorns, crushed
1–2 bay leaves, crumbled (or slivered, if using fresh)
1 tablespoon coarsely chopped garlic
4 sprigs fresh thyme, chopped
2 teaspoons whole cloves, crushed with a mortar and pestle
2 teaspoons coriander seeds, crushed with a mortar and pestle
1 cinnamon stick, crushed with a mortar and pestle

INGREDIENTS FOR THE CONFIT

8 whole cloves garlic
2–3 bay leaves
4 sprigs fresh thyme
approximately 1 quart rendered duck fat

PREPARATION

1. A minimum of 2 days in advance, but preferably 1 to 2 weeks in advance, prepare the duck legs. Divide the salt and rub into the flesh side of each leg, using all the salt specified. Combine all the remaining ingredients for the cure and rub into the flesh side of the legs. Pair legs together flesh-to-flesh and transfer to a glass or steel pan, cover, and refrigerate for 24 hours.

2. The next day, remove the duck legs and wipe off the marinade ingredients and any moisture they may have exuded. Preheat oven to 250°. Place the garlic cloves, bay leaves, and thyme in a flameproof, ovenproof deep baking pan or pot. Add the duck fat and melt over the lowest possible heat until liquid.

3. When the fat is completely melted, slip the legs into the fat, making certain they are covered by at least 1 inch. Using an instant-read or deep-frying thermometer, heat the fat over medium-low heat until it reaches 180°. Cover with foil, seal, and transfer the legs to the preheated oven.

4. Cook the legs for 45 minutes to 1 hour, or until a skewer poked at the joint produces completely clear juices. Cool the legs in the fat for an hour or so and remove them to a platter. Strain the fat into a saucepan, leaving any rendered juices behind. Bring to a simmer and cook 5 minutes, then cool.

5. Transfer the cooked duck legs to a nonreactive storage container or ceramic crock. Pour the duck fat over the legs, being certain to cover them completely. If necessary, melt more duck fat or pour peanut oil on top to cover the legs. Refrigerate.

6. The legs may be used immediately but develop greater flavor the longer they are stored. They will keep, if properly covered and refrigerated, for up to 6 months. This recipe doubles readily.

INGREDIENTS FOR THE LENTILS

¼ cup duck fat or peanut oil
½ cup onion, finely diced
½ cup carrot, finely diced
¼ cup celery, finely diced
¼ cup green bell pepper, finely diced
1 tablespoon minced fresh garlic
1 bay leaf
1 teaspoon crushed red pepper flakes
½ cup fresh tomatoes, peeled, seeded, and chopped
  (or you may substitute canned tomatoes)
1 pound green lentils de Puy
1 quart (or more) unsalted chicken stock
salt and freshly ground black pepper
2 tablespoons honey (we use sourwood)
¼ cup ketchup
¼ teaspoon Tabasco
¼ cup chopped sage
¼ cup chopped parsley

PREPARATION

1. In the duck fat, cook the onions, carrots, and celery over medium heat until softened. Add the green pepper, garlic, bay leaf, and red pepper flakes and cook for 2 minutes. Add the tomatoes, lentils, and chicken stock, bring to a boil, and then simmer until tender. You may have to add more stock depending on the age of the lentils.

2. When the lentils are tender, season with salt and pepper.

3. Combine the remaining ingredients, stir into the warm lentils, and adjust the seasoning with salt, cider vinegar, Tabasco, and/or honey to taste.

ASSEMBLY

1. Pull the duck legs from refrigeration and set them in a warm place for several hours so the fat will melt. Lift the legs from the fat, draining off the excess, and transfer to a platter.

2. Prepare the lentils and keep warm.

3. Heat 1 or 2 nonstick skillets over medium heat. Add the legs, skin-side down, and lower the heat to medium-low. Cover the pan and cook for 10 to 12 minutes, or until the skin is deep golden brown and very crisp. Be careful when lifting the lid not to let steam generated on the underside fall into the hot fat.

4. Turn the legs and cook for 2 minutes longer, until warmed through. Spoon a portion of barbecued lentils onto warm plates. Top the lentils with a duck leg and serve with piccalilli (page 178) and an arugula salad on the side.

Confit Duck Hash with Poached Eggs & Béarnaise Aioli

SERVES 8

Every once in a while, you have to say "to hell with my cholesterol count!" and fix a big, nasty brunch. We made this dish for Cuisines of the Sun at Mauna Lani Bay in Hawaii, where it was a huge hit.

You can assemble all the components for this dish a day ahead, even poach the eggs and hold them in ice water. So if you're laboring with a hangover, it won't be nearly as traumatic. Serve with Bloody Marys, or Mimosas, if you must.

INGREDIENTS FOR THE HASH

4 confit duck legs (see the preceding recipe),
   skinned, boned, and cut into ½-inch chunks
duck fat (or peanut oil)
1 medium onion, diced (about 1 cup)
1 red bell pepper, diced (about ½ cup)
1 green bell pepper, diced (about ½ cup)
2 tablespoons minced garlic
1 jalapeño, seeded and minced (optional)
½ pound sweet potatoes, peeled, cut into medium dice,
   and blanched in salted water
½ pound russet potatoes, peeled, cut into medium dice,
   and blanched in salted water
¾ cup roasted gold beets, peeled and diced (optional)
duck stock or chicken stock, if needed
¼ cup fresh thyme leaves

¼ cup tarragon vinegar

salt and black pepper to taste

INGREDIENTS FOR THE BÉARNAISE AIOLI

    2 tablespoons shallots, minced fine

    ¼ cup tarragon vinegar

    ¼ cup white wine

    1 egg yolk, at room temperature

    2 tablespoons roasted garlic purée (page 245)

    ½ cup safflower oil

    2 tablespoons tarragon, chopped

    1 tablespoon flat-leaf parsley, chopped

    salt, black pepper, Tabasco, and Worcestershire sauce to taste

INGREDIENTS FOR SERVING

    8 poached eggs (see page 30 for poaching procedure)

    ½ cup scallions, cut into ¼-inch rounds

PREPARATION

1. Remove the duck confit from the fat and crisp it, skin-side down, over medium heat. Remove, cool slightly, and remove skin. Bone the legs and cut into ½-inch chunks. Set aside.

2. In the same pan used for the legs, heat the duck fat, or peanut oil, and sauté the onions over medium heat until lightly caramelized. Remove to a plate. Cook the green and red peppers until softened and just caramelized. Add the garlic and jalapeño, cook 1 minute, and transfer to the plate with the onions.

3. Make the aioli. In a nonreactive saucepan, combine the shallots, vinegar, and wine, bring to a boil, and simmer to reduce until syrupy. Cool and scrape into the bowl of a food processor. Add the egg yolk and roasted garlic purée; pulse to combine. With the machine running, drizzle oil through the tube to emulsify. Pulse in the herbs and season with salt, pepper, Tabasco, and Worcestershire sauce to taste. Set aside, or refrigerate if not using immediately.

TO SERVE

1. Have egg poaching water and eggs ready.

2. In a large sauté pan, heat the duck fat (or oil) until shimmering. Add the blanched sweet and russet potatoes and sauté over medium-high heat until hot and the edges are beginning to brown. Add the reserved duck meat, beets (if you are using them), onions, and pepper mixture and sauté until warmed through. (Add a little duck stock if mixture seems dry.) Add the thyme leaves and tarragon vinegar, season well, and keep hot.

3. Poach the eggs to desired doneness (but the yolks should still be runny). Divide the hash between 8 hot plates, mounding it up in the center of the plate. Top the hash with a poached egg, then spoon a tablespoon of aioli on top of each egg and drizzle a little around the plate. Sprinkle with scallions and serve immediately.

Roast Squab with Blackberry Essence & Carrot-Thyme Spaetzle

SERVES 4

We have been fortunate to be able to get pigeon from our friends at Palmetto Farm in South Carolina since the restaurant's early days. We love their meaty, faintly gamey flavor and think they are wonderful juxtaposed against the sweet tartness of summer blackberries.

We recommend cooking the breast meat to medium rare, which renders the squab moist, rich, and flavorful; the leg meat benefits from the quick confit treatment to help cook it through.

Your butcher should be able to order fresh squab, or they are available from specialty suppliers such as D'Artagnan (see Sources).

An alternative to the spaetzle would be to serve the squab with one of our spoonbreads (page 168). The sweet potato variation goes particularly well with this dish.

INGREDIENTS FOR THE SQUAB

 4 whole squab, dressed (14–16 ounces each)
 salt and black pepper
 olive oil or duck fat
 1–2 sprigs fresh thyme
 2–4 tablespoons unsalted butter

INGREDIENTS FOR THE STOCK AND SAUCE

 1–2 tablespoons olive oil
 reserved wing tips and neck bones from squab
 1 cup shallots, peeled and sliced
 1 bay leaf
 3 cups roasted chicken stock (page 228)
 ¼ cup sugar
 1 cup red wine
 ½ cup red wine vinegar
 1 pint fresh blackberries
 1 teaspoon coriander seeds, lightly toasted and crushed
 2–3 juniper berries
 2 sprigs fresh thyme
 ½ teaspoon black peppercorns, cracked
 salt and black pepper to taste

INGREDIENTS FOR THE SPAETZLE

 1 recipe carrot-thyme spaetzle (page 160)
 1½ cups torn Swiss chard or spinach leaves, washed
 ½ cup carrot, cut into julienne, blanched until tender
 olive oil or duck fat
 salt and black pepper to taste

PREPARATION

1. Prepare the squab. Carefully cut the leg and thigh portions from each bird. Season liberally with salt and pepper and put in a small saucepan with olive oil or melted duck fat to cover. Bring to a simmer and cook at the lowest heat for 5 minutes. Remove from heat and cool in the oil. Reserve.

2. Cut the wing tips at the second joint and remove the neck. Refrigerate the breast portions on the bone until ready to cook. Return to room temperature before cooking.

3. Prepare the stock. In a medium saucepan, heat the olive oil and brown the wing tips and neck bones until deeply colored. Add the shallots and bay leaf and cook until the shallots are softened. Add the stock, bring to a simmer, and cook, skimming scum as it rises, until reduced by a third. Strain and set aside, or refrigerate.

4. Prepare the sauce. In a heavy-bottomed saucepan, combine the sugar, wine, and vinegar. Reserve 12 nice blackberries for garnish and add the remainder to the vinegar-sugar mixture. Bring to a boil and cook over medium heat until syrupy. Add the coriander seed, juniper berries, and reserved squab stock; bring to a simmer and cook until reduced by half. Add the thyme sprigs and cracked black pepper, remove from heat, and infuse for 5 minutes. Strain, season, and reserve.

5. Make the spaetzle and prepare the accompanying vegetables.

ASSEMBLY

1. Preheat oven to 350°. Remove the legs from the olive oil or fat and the breasts from refrigeration. Heat 1 or 2 ovenproof skillets over medium-high heat; reduce the heat to medium and add a film of olive oil, a sprig of thyme, and 1 to 2 tablespoons of butter to each pan. Roll the squab breasts in the butter and brown on all sides, basting with the butter, for about 5 minutes. Turn the squab onto their backs, breast-side up, baste again, and transfer to the oven. Roast for 5 to 7 minutes, until the breasts are medium rare. Remove to a cutting board to rest and keep warm.

2. While the squab breasts are roasting, brown the legs over medium heat on both sides. Keep warm. Reheat the sauce and keep warm.

3. Heat olive oil or duck fat in a nonstick pan. Add 2 cups of spaetzle to the pan and cook over medium heat until golden brown. Add the julienned carrot and toss the spaetzle mixture with the chard until the greens are wilted. Season and divide between 4 warm plates.

4. Cut the squab breasts away from the body, down through the joint connecting the wing to the body. Place 2 legs on top of the spaetzle and arrange 2 breast pieces in front of the spaetzle. Spoon the sauce around and garnish with the reserved whole blackberries.

Striped Bass with Oyster Stew

SERVES 6

At one time, striped bass flourished in the Pamlico Sound on North Carolina's coast. Overfishing and pollution seriously diminished the bass population, however, resulting in severe restrictions on their commercial harvest. Through better fisheries management, there has been a resurgence in the bass population on the East Coast, and we are now regularly able to offer this delicious fish at the restaurant.

This preparation accentuates the terrific crispness that can be achieved by searing the skin side first. In the fall, the fish are particularly fatty from a summer of feeding, and this method protects the flesh from overcooking and drying out.

Serve the bass with the first oysters of autumn and accompany with tomato gumbo (page 154) and Bean's black skillet cornbread (page 172).

INGREDIENTS FOR THE BASS

> 6 wild striped bass or rockfish filets (6 ounces each), skin on and scaled
> salt and freshly ground black pepper
> 1½ tablespoons unsalted butter, softened at room temperature
> peanut oil for sautéing

INGREDIENTS FOR THE STEW

> 1 pint shucked oysters
> 2 ounces country ham, sliced thin and cut into ¼-inch dice
> 2 tablespoons peanut oil
> ½ cup onion, cut into small dice
> ¼ cup red bell pepper, seeded and cut into small dice
> ¼ cup celery, cut into small dice
> 2 tablespoons garlic, minced
> ½ teaspoon crushed red pepper flakes
> 1 bay leaf
> ¼ cup bourbon
> 2 tablespoons lemon juice
> ½ cup white wine
> 1½ cups roasted chicken stock (page 228)
> 2 tablespoons heavy cream
> 2 tablespoons unsalted butter
> 1 tablespoon chopped sage
> salt, black pepper, and lemon juice to taste
> ½ cup scallions, sliced crosswise (use both white and green parts)

PREPARATION FOR THE STEW

> 1. Strain the oysters and reserve the oyster liquor; refrigerate the oysters until ready to use for final assembly. In a medium saucepan, cook the ham in the peanut oil until lightly caramelized. Add the onion, red bell pepper, and celery and cook until caramelized. Add the garlic, red pepper flakes, and bay leaf; cook 1 minute.

2. Add the bourbon, lemon juice, wine, and reserved oyster liquor. Cook until greatly reduced and nearly syrupy, stirring frequently. Add the roasted chicken stock and simmer over medium heat, skimming as necessary, until reduced by half. Cool and reserve until preparing the bass. Remove the bay leaf.

ASSEMBLY

1. Remove the bass from refrigeration and dry thoroughly with paper towels. With a sharp knife, score an X in the skin side to prevent it from curling when the fish is cooking. Season the flesh side with salt and pepper; rub the skin side with some of the softened butter.

2. If serving with tomato gumbo, heat the gumbo and stir in the cooked rice as indicated in the last step of the recipe. Keep warm. Return the stew to low heat and add the heavy cream; bring to a slow simmer.

3. Heat a large, heavy skillet over medium-high heat for 2 minutes. Add a film of peanut oil, then carefully lay the filets in the pan, skin-side down. Reduce the heat to medium and press firmly on the filets with the back of a metal spatula to flatten slightly and aid in the searing; cook 3 to 5 minutes, depending on the thickness of the filets. When the edges of the filets begin to show doneness, turn carefully and cook 1 minute longer. Remove the filets and keep warm.

4. Raise the heat on the stew to medium-high, stir in the oysters and butter, and cook just until the oysters are plumped and beginning to curl. Remove from the heat, stir in the sage, and season with salt, black pepper, and lemon juice to taste.

5. Warm 6 wide, shallow bowls. If serving with tomato gumbo, spoon ¾ cup of gumbo in the center of each bowl. Place a filet in each bowl, on top of the gumbo if used. Spoon the stew around the filets, dividing the oysters equally between the bowls. Sprinkle liberally with scallions and serve immediately.

Pan-Fried Mountain Rainbow Trout with Green Tomato & Lime Brown Butter Salsa on Sweet Potato, Artichoke, & Crawfish Hash

SERVES 4

Unless you're a fly fisherman, or hang out with one, you'll rarely encounter wild trout, which has an incomparable flavor in need of little or no augmentation. Chances are, like us, you'll be cooking farm-raised trout, which can stand more complex adornments. In a take on the classic trout beurre noisette, we created this dish for a television shoot in the kitchen.

If you're unable to find heirloom tomatoes that ripen green, just substitute more tomatillos or yellow or red tomatoes.

INGREDIENTS FOR THE TROUT

    4 butterflied rainbow trout (10 ounces each), head on
    salt and freshly ground black pepper
    ¼ cup combined chopped Italian parsley, cilantro, and oregano
    olive oil for sautéing

INGREDIENTS FOR THE HASH

    ½ cup onion, peeled and cut into ½-inch dice
    ⅓ cup red bell pepper, cut into ½-inch dice
    ⅓ cup yellow bell pepper, cut into ½-inch dice
    1 pound sweet potatoes, cut into ½-inch dice
    1 tablespoon minced garlic
    4 ounces cooked crawfish tail meat, split lengthwise,
        or cooked shrimp, cut into ½-inch dice
    ½ cup marinated baby artichokes (page 247), cut into eighths,
        or frozen artichoke bottoms, cooked and cut into wedges
    ½ cup olive oil, divided
    salt and freshly ground black pepper
    ¼ cup combined chopped Italian parsley, cilantro, and oregano

INGREDIENTS FOR THE SALSA

    ⅓ cup tomatillo, cut into ½-inch rough pieces
    ½ cup green-ripening tomato (e.g., Evergreen or Green Zebra),
        peeled, seeded, and cut into ½-inch dice
    1–2 red or green serranos, seeded and cut into fine slivers
    1 pasilla or poblano chile, roasted, peeled, seeded, and cut into julienne
    4 garlic cloves, poached in 3 changes of water until tender, sliced thin
    1 stick (4 ounces) unsalted butter, cut into 3 or 4 pieces
    2 ounces fresh-squeezed lime juice
    pinch salt
    ¼ cup combined chopped Italian parsley, cilantro, and oregano

1. For the hash: In olive oil, sauté the onion over medium heat until softened and translucent. Remove and drain the excess oil. Cook the red pepper until just softened; remove and drain. Cook the yellow pepper; remove and drain. Cool, combine the onions and peppers, and set aside.

2. For the salsa: Combine the diced tomatillo, green tomato, slivered serrano, julienned pasilla (or poblano) chile, and poached garlic. Season and set aside.

3. Preheat oven to 350°. In 1 or 2 large ovenproof sauté pans, heat olive oil over medium-high heat. Dry the trout, inside and out. Season liberally, inside and out, with salt and freshly ground black pepper and divide the herbs between the cavities. Place the trout on their sides in the sauté pan(s), reduce the heat to medium, and cook 3 minutes. Turn the trout and place the pans in the oven; cook 3 to 4 minutes, or until the flesh is barely jelled at the backbone.

4. While the trout is cooking, heat olive oil over medium-high heat in a 10-inch sauté pan. Add the raw sweet potatoes and sauté until they start to caramelize and soften. Add the onion and pepper mixture and cook 1 minute. Add the garlic and cook 30 seconds; add the crawfish tail meat and artichokes and warm through. Season generously, toss with the herbs, and divide between 4 hot platters. Put one trout on each platter beside the hash.

5. In an 8-inch sauté pan, melt the butter over high heat until past the foaming point. It will begin to brown lightly and will smell nutty. Add the lime juice and salsa and toss to warm (careful: the butter will sizzle and spatter!). Season with salt and herbs and divide the salsa over each trout. Serve hot.

Grilled Tuna with Roasted Eggplant & Cucumber Vermicelli

SERVES 6

This is a terrific entrée to serve in the warm summer months when eggplants and cucumbers are prolific. Great quality tuna can be grilled quickly and served with the room-temperature vegetable accompaniments, which have been prepared in advance. Tuna on the grill has the requisite meatiness to stand up to the powerful flavors of the accompaniments, but you may also use very fresh wahoo in its place.

INGREDIENTS FOR THE TUNA

6 tuna steaks, 1 inch thick (about 6 ounces each)

¼ cup mushroom soy sauce (see note)

2 small dried red chiles, chopped, or ½ teaspoon crushed red pepper flakes

2 tablespoons ginger, roughly chopped

4 cloves garlic, mashed

2 tablespoons chopped cilantro

2 tablespoons peanut oil

1 tablespoon sesame oil

   1 teaspoon minced ginger

   1 teaspoon minced garlic

   1 tablespoon lemon juice

   1 teaspoon rice wine vinegar

   1 egg yolk, at room temperature

   7 tablespoons peanut oil

   1 tablespoon sesame oil

   dash mushroom soy sauce

   1 tablespoon minced cilantro

INGREDIENTS FOR THE GARNISH AND ASSEMBLY

   1 recipe roasted eggplant (page 150)

   1 recipe cucumber vermicelli (page 151)

   ½ cup scallion tops, sliced thin on the bias

   1 teaspoon black sesame seeds, or white sesame seeds, lightly toasted

PREPARATION

   1. Prepare the eggplant according to the recipe directions and reserve at room temperature.

   2. Prepare the cucumber vermicelli according to the recipe directions and refrigerate until half an hour before serving.

   3. Prepare the aioli. In a small bowl, combine the ginger, garlic, lemon juice, and rice wine vinegar. Add the egg yolk and whisk to combine. Slowly whisk in the peanut and sesame oils until emulsified. Season with the soy sauce, and additional lemon if desired, and fold in the cilantro. Reserve.

   4. Light the grill, and while the coals are cooking down, combine all the ingredients for the tuna marinade. Marinate the steaks for no more than 10 to 15 minutes on each side. Remove to a plate and wipe off the excess marinade ingredients.

   5. Spoon ½ cup of eggplant into the center of each of 6 room-temperature plates. Check the seasoning of the cucumber vermicelli and mold ½ cup on top of the eggplant.

   6. Grill the tuna over medium-hot coals, about 3 minutes per side for medium rare, and remove from the fire. Cut the tuna steaks once, on the bias, and arrange next to the eggplant and cucumber vermicelli.

   7. Drizzle the tuna and plate with the aioli; sprinkle with the scallions and sesame seeds. Serve immediately, with additional aioli on the side.

Note: Mushroom soy sauce is available at Oriental markets; regular soy sauce works just as well.

Halibut in Sorrel & Lemongrass Nage
with Morels & Spring Onion–Asparagus Fondue

SERVES 8

When we were invited to cook a spring dinner with Debbie Gold and Michael Smith at American Restaurant in Kansas City, we wanted to showcase seasonal ingredients readily obtainable in the Midwest. Since all ocean fish has to be flown to Kansas City anyway and we love the delicate nature of halibut, that fish seemed an obvious choice. Even more obvious was the combination of asparagus and morels, but the lemongrass and sorrel nage provides both the link and the counterpoint for the dish. And, in truth, we always wanted to use the word "nage" in a menu description.

INGREDIENTS FOR THE HALIBUT

    3 pounds fresh halibut filet, from the thickest section of the fish, skinless
    salt and freshly ground black pepper
    olive oil for sautéing
    1 pound fresh morels, trimmed and halved or quartered if large
      (or ½ pound dried morels, reconstituted)
    2 tablespoons chives, snipped fine

INGREDIENTS FOR THE NAGE

    2 tablespoons unsalted butter + 4 tablespoons unsalted butter reserved to finish
    ½ cup minced shallots
    ¼ cup tarragon vinegar
    ¼ cup lemon juice
    1½ cups Sauvignon Blanc, or other dry white wine
    2 cups fish stock (or 10 ounces bottled clam juice
      diluted with 6 ounces chicken stock)
    1 stalk lemongrass, minced
    salt and black pepper to taste
    1 cup fresh sorrel leaves, cut into fine chiffonade
      (or substitute ⅓ cup tarragon leaves)

INGREDIENTS FOR THE SPRING ONION–ASPARAGUS FONDUE

    1 pound thin asparagus, stemmed
    2 tablespoons whole, unsalted butter + 4 tablespoons unsalted butter reserved
    1 pound spring onions, white part and pale green stems only, sliced thin
    zest of 1 lemon, grated
    salt and black pepper to taste
    ¼ cup chopped flat-leaf parsley
    2 tablespoons minced fresh tarragon

PREPARATION FOR THE HALIBUT AND NAGE

    1. Cut the halibut into 6-ounce blocky portions and refrigerate until 20 minutes before cooking. Dry thoroughly on both sides with clean towels and set aside.

2. For the nage: Melt 2 tablespoons butter in a nonreactive pan. Add the shallots and stew over medium heat 3 minutes, until softened but not colored. Add the vinegar, lemon juice, and wine, bring to a boil, and reduce to ¼ cup. Add the fish stock, bring to a simmer, and cook slowly for 15 minutes, skimming any impurities, until reduced to about 1 cup. Add the lemongrass, infuse for 15 minutes, season, and strain into a clean saucepot. Reserve.

PREPARATION FOR THE FONDUE

1. Snap off the woody bottom of each asparagus spear and discard. Cut the tips from the asparagus, blanch the tips in salted water until crisp-tender, cool in ice water, drain, and reserve for garnish.

2. Cut the tender asparagus stems in ⅛-inch rounds and reserve; you should have about 1 cup.

3. In a heavy-bottomed saucepot, melt 2 tablespoons butter until foaming over medium heat. Add the spring onions and stew, covered, over medium-low heat, stirring occasionally, until very soft. Stir in the cut asparagus stems and cook, stirring, 3 to 5 minutes, until the asparagus is tender.

4. Transfer the asparagus and spring onion mix to the bowl of a food processor or blender and purée, scraping down the sides, until smooth. With the machine running, add 4 tablespoons of butter, cut into pieces, until emulsified. Add the lemon zest, season, and cool. When cool, add the herbs and reserve at room temperature.

FINAL PREPARATION AND ASSEMBLY

1. In a heavy-bottomed sauté pan, heat olive oil over medium-high heat and sauté the morels quickly until tender. Season, drain any excess liquid, and reserve warm.

2. Heat 1 or 2 large steel sauté pans over medium-high heat. Season the halibut generously, add olive oil to the pan(s), and sear the halibut for 2 minutes, until golden brown. Turn the halibut, reduce the heat to medium, and cook 2 to 3 minutes on the second side until just gelled (or to desired doneness).

3. While the halibut is cooking, rewarm the nage over medium heat. Off the heat, swirl in the reserved 4 tablespoons of butter and adjust the seasoning. Keep warm.

4. Put ⅓ cup of spring onion–asparagus fondue in the center of each of 8 warm wide, flat bowls. Divide the asparagus tips, morels, and sorrel chiffonade around the fondue. Place the halibut on top of the fondue and spoon nage around and over the vegetables. Sprinkle with chives and serve immediately.

Pan-Seared Red Snapper with Lobster Tomato Sauce & Gazpacho Garnish

SERVES 4

One of our fishmongers, Steve Strouse, has been bringing us native fish since our days at the Fearrington House. When he tells us he has beautiful B-Liners (a strain of red snapper from the Gulfstream), we usually buy them because they cook up beautifully and our guests love them.

This presentation borrows from traditional gazpacho, with tomatoes and crunchy vegetables, while the lobster stock adds an additional nuance and sweetness to the broth. Although it is served warm, the broth still has a freshness and vibrancy, and, served with saffron rice, this is a beautiful and complete dish.

INGREDIENTS FOR THE SNAPPER

    4 red snapper filets (6 ounces each), trimmed and scaled, with skin on
    Wondra flour (optional; see note)
    salt and black pepper to taste
    olive oil for sautéing

INGREDIENTS FOR THE SAUCE

    3 tablespoons olive oil
    ½ yellow onion, sliced thin
    3 cloves garlic, sliced thin
    1 bay leaf
    1 teaspoon coriander seed
    ½ teaspoon anise seed
    1 teaspoon paprika
    small pinch crushed red pepper flakes
    ½ pound very ripe red tomatoes, peeled, seeded, and coarsely chopped
    2 tablespoons sherry vinegar
    ¼ cup tarragon vinegar
    ½ cup dry sherry
    ½ cup white wine
    2 cups lobster stock (page 232)
    salt, black pepper, and Tabasco to taste
    2 tablespoons tarragon leaves, minced
    2 tablespoons extra virgin olive oil

INGREDIENTS FOR THE HERB AIOLI

    1 egg yolk
    1 clove garlic, minced
    2 tablespoons sherry vinegar
    ½ cup olive oil
    1 tablespoon minced tarragon
    1 tablespoon chopped flat-leaf parsley
    salt and black pepper to taste

INGREDIENTS FOR THE GARNISH

1 tablespoon zucchini skin, blanched, plunged into ice water, drained, and diced fine

1 tablespoon raw cucumber, peeled, seeded, and diced fine

1 tablespoon red bell pepper, peeled, seeded, and diced fine

1 tablespoon yellow bell pepper, peeled, seeded, and diced fine

1 tablespoon fava beans, blanched, plunged into ice water, drained, peeled, and diced fine

PREPARATION FOR THE SAUCE

1. In a saucepot over medium heat, cook the onion in the olive oil until softened but not colored. Add the sliced garlic and the bay leaf; cook 2 minutes. Grind the coriander and anise seeds in a spice mill or with a mortar and pestle. Add to the onions and garlic, along with the paprika and red pepper flakes, and cook 1 minute.

2. Add the tomatoes, sherry vinegar, tarragon vinegar, sherry, and wine. Bring to a simmer and cook, stirring frequently, until reduced by half. Add the lobster stock, bring to a simmer, and cook gently for 10 minutes.

3. Remove the bay leaf and pulse the sauce in a blender, then press it through a fine strainer. Discard the solids and reserve the sauce.

PREPARATION FOR THE HERB AIOLI

In a bowl, whisk together the egg yolk, garlic, and vinegar. Slowly drizzle in the oil, whisking constantly, until emulsified and all the oil is incorporated. Fold in the herbs and season to taste. Reserve. Refrigerate if not using immediately.

ASSEMBLY

1. Combine the garnish ingredients. Reserve.

2. Warm the sauce over low heat and season. Adjust the acidity with more vinegar if the tomatoes are very sweet; the sauce should be brothy and fairly tart. Stir in the tarragon leaves and extra virgin olive oil. Keep warm.

3. Heat 1 large or 2 medium-sized heavy-bottomed sauté pans over medium-high heat. Dry the fish filets thoroughly on cloth towels and season the flesh side of each with salt and pepper. Sprinkle the skin side with Wondra flour, if you wish to use it.

4. Film the sauté pan(s) with olive oil and lay the filets inside, skin-side down. Sear on medium-high heat for 1 minute, pressing on the filets to brown the skin evenly. Reduce the heat to medium and cook until the filets begin to look done on the edges. Turn and cook 30 seconds longer on the flesh side.

5. Place the snapper filets in 4 warm wide, shallow bowls, skin-side up (and on top of saffron rice, if you wish). Spoon lobster tomato sauce around the filets and spoon a big dollop of aioli on top of each filet. Sprinkle the gazpacho garnish liberally over the fish and sauce. Serve immediately.

Note: Wondra flour is the trade name of a finely milled flour and cornstarch product that is useful for browning and sautéing.

Grilled Sturgeon on Wild Rice Risotto with Butternuts, Grilled Leeks, & Cider Reduction

SERVES 6

This dish appears on our menu in no small part because we were introduced to the producers of Belusa farmed sturgeon and Lundberg rices at the American Harvest Workshop at Cakebread Winery in Napa Valley. Wild sturgeon once was commercially fished in North and South Carolina rivers but, unfortunately, pollution has eliminated that resource. Farm-raised fish has a wonderfully firm, meaty texture that makes it a delicious alternative to swordfish, an overfished species that deserves to be allowed to regenerate. The Lundberg family in California produces a broad range of specialty rices; we are particularly fond of their nutty wild rice blend.

Texturally complex and visually dramatic, this plate is a lovely fall seafood preparation. At the restaurant, we top the fish with a small salad of watercress, julienned apple, toasted walnuts, and haricots verts tossed in a cider-walnut vinaigrette.

INGREDIENTS FOR THE STURGEON AND MARINADE

6 sturgeon filets (6 ounces each), skinless
1 tablespoon coriander seed, coarsely crushed
1 teaspoon caraway seed, coarsely crushed
zest of 1 lemon, grated
1 tablespoon sage leaves, minced + 1 tablespoon sage leaves,
   cut into chiffonade for garnish
¼ cup olive oil
salt and black pepper
sage oil (page 241; optional)

INGREDIENTS FOR THE RISOTTO

2 tablespoons olive oil
2 tablespoons unsalted butter
½ cup onion, cut into small dice
½ cup carrot, cut into small dice
½ cup butternut squash, cut into small dice
1 tablespoon garlic, minced
2 bay leaves
1½ cups wild rice blend
¼ cup long-grain wild rice
1 cup apple cider
3½ cups chicken stock + ½ cup for finishing
1 teaspoon salt
2 baby leeks, trimmed and washed
   (or substitute 1 tender, medium-sized leek, split lengthwise)
½ cup Granny Smith apple, peeled, cut into small dice,
   and held in acidulated water

reserved meat from ham hock (optional; see below)

2 tablespoons fresh sage, chopped

2 tablespoons flat-leaf parsley, chopped

2–4 tablespoons unsalted butter, cut into pieces (if desired)

salt and black pepper to taste

INGREDIENTS FOR THE CIDER REDUCTION

¼ cup olive oil

1 small smoked ham hock (optional)

1 cup onion, cut into medium dice

1 carrot, peeled and cut into chunks

2 ribs celery, cut into medium dice

1 Granny Smith apple, cut into chunks

1 tablespoon coriander seed, crushed

1 teaspoon caraway seed, crushed

4 cloves garlic, crushed

2 bay leaves

½ cup cider vinegar

1 cup apple cider

1 cup white wine

1½ quarts roasted chicken stock (page 228)

2 tablespoons roasted garlic purée (page 245)

salt and black pepper to taste

INGREDIENTS FOR THE BUTTERNUT COULIS

½ cup Granny Smith apple, peeled and cut into pieces

1 cup butternut squash, peeled and cut into ½-inch pieces

¼ cup cider vinegar

½ cup white port (or Lillet)

2 tablespoons Applejack brandy (optional)

pinch saffron

½ cup chicken stock

1 tablespoon roasted garlic purée (page 245)

¼ cup olive oil

salt and black pepper to taste

PREPARATION FOR THE CIDER REDUCTION

1. In a heavy-bottomed pot, heat the olive oil over medium-high heat and brown the ham hock on all sides, if using. Add the onion, carrot, and celery; cook until caramelized. Add the apple, coriander seed, caraway seed, garlic, and bay leaves; cook 1 minute.

2. Add the cider vinegar, cider, and wine, bring to a simmer, and cook until reduced by three-quarters. Add the roasted chicken stock, bring to a simmer, and cook until reduced by two-thirds. Strain into a clean saucepan, reserving the ham hock. Cook the sauce down to about 1 cup, skimming as necessary.

3. Stir in the roasted garlic purée, season with salt and pepper, and adjust the acidity with cider vinegar. Strain and keep warm (or cool and refrigerate, then reheat before proceeding with the recipe).

4. Cut the lean meat from the ham hock (if using) and dice fine. Reserve for finishing the risotto.

PREPARATION FOR THE RISOTTO

1. In a heavy-bottomed pot, heat the olive oil with the butter over medium heat. Add the onion and carrot and cook until softened without browning. Add the butternut squash, garlic, and bay leaves; cook 2 minutes. Add the wild rice blend and long-grain wild rice and stir to coat with butter and oil. Add the cider, bring to a boil, and add 3½ cups chicken stock and 1 teaspoon salt. Bring to a simmer, cover, and cook gently over low heat for 30 minutes, or until the rice is tender but still firm. Spread on a pan to cool (may be prepared ahead to this point). Reserve.

2. Blanch the leek(s) in salted water until tender. Drain, cool in ice water, and drain thoroughly. Toss the leek(s) in just enough olive oil to coat them. Reserve.

PREPARATION FOR THE BUTTERNUT COULIS

1. Combine the apple, butternut squash, cider vinegar, white port, brandy, and saffron in a nonreactive saucepan. Bring to a boil and simmer until the liquid is reduced to a syrup. Add the chicken stock, bring to a boil, and transfer to a blender.

2. Add the roasted garlic purée to the blender and blend until smooth. With the blender running, drizzle olive oil into the purée, season, and reserve at room temperature.

ASSEMBLY

1. Light the grill and let the coals cook down to medium-hot. Grill the leek(s) until lightly charred and then cut into ½-inch pieces; set aside. Return the rice to the pot with ½ cup of chicken stock and warm over medium heat until hot. Drain the diced apple and stir it in, along with the leek(s) and the meat from the ham hock (if using). Finish with the herbs and butter, season, and keep warm. Rewarm the cider reduction.

2. To marinate the sturgeon, combine the coriander seed, caraway seed, lemon zest, minced sage, and olive oil. Press the filets, presentation-side *only*, into the marinade. Season liberally with salt and pepper and grill on the marinated side until crusty and lightly charred, about 3 minutes. Turn and finish cooking until the fish is firm but still juicy, about 3 minutes longer.

3. Divide the wild rice risotto between 6 warm plates. Spoon butternut coulis around the risotto on each plate and place a sturgeon filet on the risotto. Spoon the cider reduction around the butternut coulis, drizzle on a teaspoon of sage oil if desired, and sprinkle with sage chiffonade. Serve immediately.

Schoolkids' Flounder with Fish Camp Beurre Blanc

SERVES 4

Impeccably fresh fish, fried crisp and served with slaw and tartar sauce, is an integral part of Ben's childhood restaurant memories. Family excursions to the Sanitary Fish Market in Morehead City, North Carolina, live on in this presentation, inspired by an unusual circumstance.

Schoolchildren from the North Carolina Outer Banks were embarking on a cross-state bus tour to the mountains. To help finance the trip, their fisherman fathers had donated a day's catch, and their teacher called the restaurant to see if we would be interested in buying the fish. On a whim, we said yes, and at 5:30 P.M., a big yellow schoolbus pulled into our parking lot and unloaded some of the freshest, shiniest flounder we had ever seen. Our guests were the lucky ones that night.

To completely capture the essence of this plate, serve it with spicy coleslaw (page 156) and hushpuppies (page 174).

INGREDIENTS FOR THE BEURRE BLANC

> 2 tablespoons shallots, minced
>
> ¼ cup cider vinegar
>
> ¼ cup lemon juice
>
> 1 cup white wine
>
> 1 cup fish stock or chicken stock
>
> 1 tablespoon heavy cream
>
> 8 tablespoons unsalted butter, cut into pieces, chilled
>
> 1 tablespoon chopped capers
>
> 2 tablespoons minced cornichons
>
> zest of 1 lemon, grated
>
> 1 tablespoon chopped tarragon
>
> 1 tablespoon chopped flat-leaf parsley
>
> salt, black pepper, and Tabasco to taste

PREPARATION

1. Combine the shallots, vinegar, lemon juice, and wine in a nonreactive saucepot. Bring to a simmer and cook until reduced to nearly nothing, almost syrupy. Add the stock and reduce to about ¼ cup.

2. Add the cream, bring to a simmer, and reduce the heat to medium-low. Whisk in the butter, one piece at a time, incorporating each before adding the next, until all the butter is added.

3. Remove from the heat and stir in the capers, cornichons, lemon zest, tarragon, and parsley. Season to taste with salt, black pepper, and Tabasco. Keep warm but do not hold over direct heat.

INGREDIENTS FOR THE FLOUNDER

> 4 6-ounce flounder filets, skin on, preferably from large or jumbo flounder
>
> 1 cup cornmeal for dredging
>
> salt, black pepper, and cayenne pepper to taste
>
> peanut oil for frying

1. Put the cornmeal in a flat baking pan and season it generously with salt, freshly ground black pepper, and cayenne to taste. Pat the flounder filets dry and make a shallow X in the skin with a sharp knife (this helps prevent the filets from curling when they hit the pan). Press the flesh side of the filets into the cornmeal mixture to coat.

2. Heat 1 or 2 large skillets over medium-high heat. Add peanut oil to a depth of ¼ inch. Shake excess cornmeal off a filet and carefully place in hot oil, coated-side down, laying the filet away from you to avoid splashing the oil. Repeat with the remaining filets and cook until golden brown on one side. Using a spatula, carefully turn the filets and cook 30 to 60 seconds longer.

3. Lift the filets from the oil and briefly drain on a brown paper bag or a cloth towel. Transfer to warm plates and spoon the beurre blanc around the fish. Serve immediately, with lemon wedges and Tabasco on the side if desired.

Salmon Choucroute in Creamy Mustard Sauce

SERVES 6

We love the flavors of Alsatian choucroute, especially on a cool winter evening. This classic dish of sausage, pork, and sauerkraut marries well with the richness of salmon. We prefer the fattier farm-raised Atlantic salmon for this preparation and recommend you use the best quality sauerkraut in glass jars. Do not use canned sauerkraut at any cost. All the components may be prepared ahead of time and then the choucroute warmed and the salmon sautéed at the last minute. Grab a bottle of luscious Alsatian or Austrian Riesling and enjoy.

INGREDIENTS FOR THE SALMON

    6 skinless salmon filets (6 ounces each)

    1½ teaspoons whole mustard seeds

    1½ teaspoons black peppercorns, cracked

    1 teaspoon coarse sea salt

    safflower oil

    2 tablespoons roughly chopped flat-leaf parsley for garnish

INGREDIENTS FOR THE CHOUCROUTE

    4 ounces country bacon, cut into ¼-inch dice

    ¼ pound garlic sausage, cut in half lengthwise and sliced into ½-inch pieces

    1 cup shallots, cut into ¼-inch dice

    ½ cup garlic, whole cloves sliced thin crosswise

    2 bay leaves

    1 teaspoon whole mustard seeds, lightly toasted and coarsely ground in a spice mill or with a mortar and pestle

    1 teaspoon whole caraway seeds, lightly toasted and coarsely ground in a spice mill or with a mortar and pestle

½ teaspoon whole coriander seeds, lightly toasted and coarsely ground
   in a spice mill or with a mortar and pestle

3 cups sauerkraut, drained, rinsed, and squeezed dry

1 cup white wine, ideally Riesling

1 cup chicken stock or water

½ pound fingerling or very small Yukon Gold potatoes,
   blanched in salted water and sliced into rounds

¼ cup chopped parsley

2 teaspoons fresh thyme leaves

salt and black pepper to taste

2 tablespoons whole butter, cut into pieces (optional)

INGREDIENTS FOR THE SAUCE

½ cup sour cream

1 tablespoon Dijon mustard

2 tablespoons coarse-grain mustard

2 tablespoons milk, or more as needed

1–2 tablespoons lemon juice to taste

salt and black pepper to taste

PREPARATION FOR THE CHOUCROUTE

1. In a heavy pan, partially render the bacon over medium-low heat until golden but not crisp. Remove to drain, leaving the renderings in the pan. Add the sausage and cook until browned but still moist and juicy. Remove to drain, again reserving the renderings.

2. In the renderings, cook the shallots over medium-low heat until softened, stirring to scrape up any bits of meat. Add the garlic slices, bay leaves, and ground spices and cook until the garlic softens, about 3 minutes.

3. Add the drained sauerkraut, white wine, and chicken stock and bring to a simmer. Cook over low heat for 30 minutes, stirring occasionally. Add more stock or water if necessary; the mixture should be moist but not soupy. The choucroute may be prepared ahead to this point.

4. Stir in the blanched potatoes, sausage, and bacon, and heat through. Add the herbs and adjust the seasoning. Stir in the butter if desired. Keep warm.

PREPARATION FOR THE SAUCE

In a small stainless bowl, stir together the sour cream and both mustards to combine. Stir in the milk to loosen to a saucelike consistency. Season with lemon juice, salt, and pepper and set aside at room temperature.

PREPARATION FOR THE SALMON

1. Heat 1 or 2 heavy sauté pans that will be large enough to accommodate the salmon filets without crowding over medium heat for 2 to 3 minutes. Combine the mustard seeds, cracked pepper, and sea salt on a plate and press the presentation side of the salmon filets into the spices to coat.

2. Add oil to the hot pans and place the salmon filets, crusted-side down, in the pans and sear for 3 minutes. Carefully turn the filets and cook for 3 minutes longer for medium rare to medium.

3. Divide the choucroute between 6 hot plates or large bowls and top with salmon filets, crusted-side up. Drizzle with the mustard sauce and sprinkle with parsley. Serve immediately.

Summer Shell Bean Minestra with Tomato Bruschetta

SERVES 8

Inspired by the Italian model, this is a wonderful vegetable stew to make when field peas, butterbeans, corn, and tomatoes are all at their peak. Make the vegetable stock a day in advance, collect all the other ingredients at your farmers' market, and sit down to a big bowlful of summer.

INGREDIENTS FOR THE MINESTRA

    4 tablespoons olive oil

    1 bay leaf

    2 leeks, trimmed, quartered, cleaned, and sliced crosswise

    1 medium onion, diced

    1 small fennel bulb, diced

    1 medium red bell pepper, diced

    2 tablespoons garlic, minced

    $\frac{1}{2}$ teaspoon fennel seed, crushed

    $\frac{1}{4}$ teaspoon crushed red pepper flakes

    2 cups fresh (or frozen) tiny lima beans

    1 cup fresh (or frozen) field peas or black-eyed peas

    5 cups vegetable stock (page 233) + a little more stock to thin if necessary

    8 ounces fresh chanterelles or shiitake mushrooms, trimmed and sliced

    4 whole ears corn, preferably Silver Queen, shucked, kernels cut off the cob, and cobs scraped, with kernels and cob scrapings reserved

    1 cup tomato concassé (page 237)

    $\frac{1}{2}$ cup flat-leaf parsley, chopped

    $\frac{1}{2}$ cup fresh basil leaves, chopped

    salt and black pepper to taste

PREPARATION

1. In a heavy nonreactive pot, heat the olive oil over medium heat. Add the bay leaf, leeks, onion, fennel, and red bell pepper. Cook, covered, over low heat until softened. Raise the heat to medium and stir in the garlic, fennel seed, and red pepper flakes. Cook 1 minute.

2. Add the limas, field peas, and vegetable stock. Bring to a boil, skim, and reduce to a simmer. Cook until the beans are tender.

3. While the beans are cooking, sauté the mushrooms in olive oil until cooked through. Reserve.

4. When the beans are done, stir in the corn, with the cob scrapings, and mushrooms; simmer 3 to 4 minutes. (The minestra may be prepared ahead to this point.) Season generously with salt and freshly ground black pepper.

INGREDIENTS FOR THE BRUSCHETTA

    8 slices semolina baguette, grilled or toasted and rubbed with garlic and olive oil

    3–4 very ripe tomatoes, peeled, seeded, and chopped

2 tablespoons basil, chopped

salt, black pepper, and olive oil to taste

PREPARATION

Combine the tomatoes, basil, salt, pepper, and olive oil; spread on the toast.

INGREDIENTS FOR SERVING

extra virgin olive oil

shaved Sonoma Dry Jack or Asiago cheese

TO SERVE

1. Heat the minestra over medium heat. Add more vegetable stock if the minestra is too thick. Stir in the tomato concassé and herbs. Check the seasoning.

2. Ladle into bowls, drizzle with a little extra virgin olive oil, garnish with shaved cheese, and serve with tomato bruschetta alongside.

Fried Green Tomato Sandwich on Buttermilk Bread with Arugula, Country Bacon, & Black Pepper Aioli

SERVES 4

No, we don't serve sandwiches at the Grill, but Ben's late-night after-work supper is often a sandwich that eats like a meal.

Here are the obligatory fried green tomatoes without which any dyed-in-the-wool Southern cookbook would be incomplete. This contemporary twist on the BLT is savory, punchy, and a little messy, but oh so good with a beer, homemade potato chips, and bread 'n butter pickles.

INGREDIENTS FOR THE SANDWICH

    8 slices buttermilk bread (page 173), cut ½ inch thick

    8 slices cured country bacon, cooked crisp (renderings reserved)

    8–12 slices (depending on diameter) firm, unripe green tomato, ½ inch thick

    ⅔ cup buttermilk

    1 cup coarse-ground cornmeal

    2 tablespoons flour

    1 teaspoon salt

    1 teaspoon freshly ground black pepper

    ½ teaspoon cayenne pepper

    ½ teaspoon dried oregano, crumbled

    1 cup peanut oil

    1 bunch arugula, stemmed and washed

INGREDIENTS FOR THE AIOLI

    1 egg yolk, at room temperature

    2 tablespoons fresh lemon juice

    2 cloves garlic, mashed to a paste with ¼ teaspoon salt

    1 teaspoon coarsely crushed black peppercorns

    1 teaspoon Dijon mustard

    ½ cup peanut oil

PREPARATION

1. Make the bread (can be made 24 hours in advance). Slice and toast lightly.
2. Cook the bacon over medium-low heat until crisp. Drain on paper toweling. Strain and reserve the rendered fat.
3. Slice the tomatoes; place in the buttermilk and refrigerate.
4. Make the aioli. Combine the egg yolk, lemon juice, garlic, pepper, and mustard. Whisk in the oil until emulsified. Adjust the seasoning and refrigerate (can be made 24 hours in advance).
5. For the tomatoes: To make the coating, combine the cornmeal, flour, salt, pepper, cayenne, and oregano. Drain the tomatoes, dredge in the cornmeal mixture to coat, and shake off the excess. The tomatoes should be completely coated.

6. Heat the peanut oil and reserved bacon renderings over medium heat (preferably in a cast-iron skillet) until shimmering. Fry the tomatoes, in batches if necessary, until crisp and golden, turning them once. Drain on brown paper bags and keep warm in a low oven.

7. For each sandwich, slather aioli on one side of two pieces of the toasted bread. Top one slice of bread with slices of tomato, 2 slices of bacon, arugula leaves, and another slice of bread. Cut crosswise, secure with frilly toothpicks, and serve immediately.

side dishes, relishes, & breads

Slow-Cooked Southern Greens

Roasted Eggplant

Cucumber Vermicelli

Blue Lake Beans with Red Wine
    Sweet Onion Pickle

Stewed Okra (a.k.a. Tomato Gumbo)

Spicy Slaw

Green Corn Pudding

"Dixie Polenta" (i.e., Creamy Roasted Garlic Grits)

Luxe Macaroni & Cheese

Carrot-Thyme Spaetzle

Buttermilk Mashed New Potatoes

Molasses Mashed Sweet Potatoes

Sweet Potato & Leek Gratin

Sweet Potato Salad

Crawfish Jambalaya Risotto

Wild Mushroom Bread Pudding

Carolina Grits Soufflé

Spoonbread

Squash Casserole

Bean's Black Skillet Cornbread

Buttermilk Bread

Buttermilk Herb Crackers

Hushpuppies

Angel Biscuits

Abundance Plum Chutney

Green Tomato Butter

Piccalilli

Iowa Corn Relish

Pickled Pepper Relish

Slow-Cooked Southern Greens

SERVES 8 AS A SIDE DISH, WITH LEFTOVERS, MAYBE

Indulge us a moment while we climb up on our soapbox. Southern-style cooked greens should be braised slowly until tender and should always be cooked with a piece of pork and some hot peppers and finished with or served with vinegar. Cornbread is only nominally optional. With all due respect to the butter or olive oil school of thought that permits crunchy-textured greens, this is the way we were raised.

We generally prefer a mixture of young turnip greens and curly mustard greens. Collards, picked after the first heavy frost, are righteous but do demand a powerful exhaust fan and a tolerance for that "cabbagey" aroma.

INGREDIENTS

7 pounds young mustard, turnip, or collard greens

6 ounces side meat (see note), cut into ¼-inch dice

2 cups onions, cut into ¼-inch dice

4 cloves garlic, minced

½ teaspoon crushed red pepper flakes or 2 small diced chiles

chicken stock or water

salt and black pepper

cider vinegar

PREPARATION

1. Clean the greens. They may be sandy and require 2 or 3 washings. Trim the stems and remove the ribs *if the greens are quite mature*. Drain thoroughly.

2. In a 4-quart, heavy-bottomed pot, cook the side meat over medium heat until rendered and golden brown. Add the onion and cook until translucent but not colored. Stir in the garlic and red pepper flakes or diced chiles, and cook for 1 minute.

3. Working in batches, add large handfuls of greens to the pot, stirring to wilt. When all the greens have been wilted, add chicken stock or water to come up to the level of the greens. Bring to a boil, then reduce to a simmer. Cook 20 to 40 minutes for mustard or turnip greens or 40 to 90 minutes for collards. Add more stock or water as necessary. The age of the greens determines the cooking time; they should be tender but still somewhat resilient.

4. Season with salt, pepper, and a liberal lacing of cider vinegar. Serve immediately, or cool and then refrigerate. Rewarm over low heat.

Note: Side meat, or "streak o' lean," is black pepper–cured, unsmoked belly bacon. Country-style slab bacon or regular bacon may be substituted.

Roasted Eggplant

YIELDS ABOUT 3 CUPS; SERVES 6 TO 8

Roasted eggplant has a supple texture, and, when treated as in this recipe, it also possesses an exotic flavor without being greasy. This recipe utilizes ordinary globe eggplant, but you may substitute Japanese eggplant or any of the "new" old-fashioned white, purple, or green varieties; just adjust the roasting time for the size of the eggplant you choose. Regardless of type, the eggplant should be smooth, glossy, and firm; if you prefer the elongated Japanese style, it isn't necessary to remove the seeds.

The pronounced flavors of fish sauce and tamarind are important to this dish; if you want, however, you may substitute soy sauce for the fish sauce and rice wine vinegar for the tamarind.

INGREDIENTS

1½ pounds eggplant
¼ cup fish sauce (available at Oriental markets)
3 tablespoons brown sugar
1 tablespoon lime juice (or more to taste)
1 tablespoon tamarind concentrate (available at Oriental markets)
1 tablespoon minced ginger
1 tablespoon minced garlic
1–2 serrano chiles, seeded and chopped
2 scallions, cut into ½-inch pieces on the bias
2 tablespoons peanut oil + peanut oil for sautéing
salt to taste
2 tablespoons cilantro, chopped

PREPARATION

1. Preheat oven to 350°. Prick the eggplant with a fork 3 or 4 times and roast on a baking sheet for 30 to 40 minutes, or until tender. Split lengthwise and cool, cut-side down, on the baking sheet. When cool enough to handle, peel and seed the eggplant. Cut the flesh into 1½- to 2-inch strips and reserve.

2. Combine the fish sauce, brown sugar, lime juice, and tamarind concentrate in a bowl and set aside. Heat a large skillet over medium-high heat, add a film of peanut oil, and sauté the ginger, garlic, chiles, and scallions for 1 minute, until aromatic. Add the liquid ingredients and bring to a boil. Stir in the eggplant and heat through; stir in the peanut oil and cool to room temperature. Season, stir in the cilantro, and serve at room temperature.

Cucumber Vermicelli

YIELDS ABOUT 2½ CUPS

This delightful "salad" is spicy and refreshing simultaneously. The textural interplay of the vegetables and bean thread noodles makes this an interesting accompaniment to grilled fish.

INGREDIENTS

1 European cucumber, peeled and seeded
1 teaspoon salt
1 bundle (¾-ounce) bean thread noodles (see note)
½ cup carrot, peeled and cut into fine julienne
½ cup red bell pepper, stemmed and seeded, cut into fine julienne
2 tablespoons lime juice
2 tablespoons rice wine vinegar
1 tablespoon minced garlic
1 tablespoon minced ginger
1 teaspoon Chinese chile paste (see note), or to taste
2 tablespoons peanut oil
dash sesame oil
dash fish sauce (see note) or soy sauce, to taste
2 tablespoons chopped cilantro

PREPARATION

1. Using a mandoline or a Japanese mandoline, cut the cucumber into long "noodles." Transfer to a colander set over a bowl, toss with the salt, and set aside for 30 minutes to leach out the juices. Squeeze gently to extract excess liquid and transfer to a clean bowl.

2. Heat 1 cup of water to just under a boil. Put the bean thread noodles in a heat-resistant container and pour hot water over them. Reconstitute the noodles for 4 to 5 minutes, until tender. Drain well and snip into manageable lengths with scissors. Combine with the cucumber "noodles" and add the julienned carrot and pepper.

3. Combine the remaining ingredients other than the cilantro and toss with the vegetables and noodles. Marinate for 1 hour, refrigerated. Toss with the cilantro and adjust the seasoning with rice wine vinegar, sesame oil, and fish sauce to taste.

Note: Bean thread noodles are available in pink net bags containing packets of 8. Chinese chile paste, or sambal, and Thai fish sauce are available at Oriental markets.

Blue Lake Beans with Red Wine Sweet Onion Pickle

SERVES 8 TO 10

Vinegar-marinated cucumbers and onions were always on the summer table in Alamance County, where Ben's grandparents lived. We would spoon them over slow-cooked pole beans cooked with a piece of pork or over sliced tomatoes, still warm from the garden. This bean salad captures some of the same flavors and is a breeze to prepare in advance. Do not marinate more than a half hour before serving, as the beans will discolor.

INGREDIENTS FOR THE RED WINE SWEET ONION PICKLE

2 pounds Bermuda, Vidalia, or red onions, peeled and sliced thin
⅔ cup red wine vinegar
⅔ cup red wine
10 black peppercorns, crushed
2 bay leaves
1 teaspoon salt

PREPARATION

1. Combine all of the ingredients except the onions and bring to a boil.
2. Pour over the sliced onions and steep for 1 hour or overnight.

INGREDIENTS FOR THE BEANS

2 pounds young, tender Blue Lake or Kentucky Wonder green beans, stemmed
salt
1 European cucumber, seeded, quartered lengthwise and sliced,
  and salted and drained for 1 hour
¼ cup peanut oil

PREPARATION

1. Bring salted water to a boil. Add the beans and cook until tender. Plunge the beans into ice water to stop cooking. Drain.
2. Toss the cucumber with the onion pickle and peanut oil. Toss the beans with the onion-cucumber mixture and add salt to taste. Marinate 30 minutes and serve at cool room temperature.

Stewed Okra (a.k.a. Tomato Gumbo)

SERVES 8 TO 10 OR MORE, DEPENDING ON YOUR QUOTA
OF OKRA LOVERS

When we served this as part of a smoked pork tenderloin plate, the menu description "stewed okra" seemed to deter a sizable percentage of customers. But once we changed the name to "tomato gumbo," the dish became amazingly popular. We also halve this recipe to serve as a starch alongside striped bass with oyster stew (page 124).

INGREDIENTS

- 2 tablespoons olive oil
- 2 tablespoons rendered bacon fat
- 2 medium onions, peeled and diced fine
- 4 cloves garlic, chopped fine
- ½ teaspoon crushed red pepper flakes
- 2 bay leaves
- 3 cups tomatoes, peeled, seeded, and coarsely chopped (or use canned tomatoes), with juices
- 2 pounds okra, sliced into ½-inch rounds
- salt and black pepper to taste
- 2 cups cooked long-grain white rice

PREPARATION

1. Heat the olive oil and bacon fat in a medium-sized skillet over medium heat. Add the onion, lower the heat, and cook, stirring occasionally, until the onion softens but doesn't color.
2. Add the garlic, red pepper flakes, and bay leaves and cook for 1 minute.
3. Add the tomatoes; add their reserved juices, as needed, to bring to a stewlike consistency and then bring the mixture to a simmer.
4. Add the okra and simmer until the okra is tender (approximately 8 to 10 minutes). Season. Stir in the cooked rice and serve immediately.

Spicy Slaw

Slaw is like fried chicken: everyone's mama's was the best. This version is subtly sweet from the red pepper, decidedly spicy, and should be balanced with a vinegary tang. If you want to make the slaw less spicy, seed the jalapeño before grinding or eliminate it entirely. The slaw should be dressed at least 1 hour before serving to blend the flavors. Serve with schoolkids' flounder (page 137), smoked pork tenderloin (page 88), or as part of a Southern vegetable plate.

INGREDIENTS

1 medium head green cabbage, trimmed, quartered, and cored

2 carrots, peeled and cut into fine julienne

1 small red bell pepper, seeded and cored, cut into chunks

1 jalapeño, sliced (with seeds optional)

2 cloves garlic, peeled

3 tablespoons cider vinegar

1 teaspoon mustard seed, ground in a spice mill

1 teaspoon celery seed, ground in a spice mill

2 teaspoons salt, or more to taste

pinch sugar

pinch cayenne pepper

¼ cup safflower or canola oil

2 tablespoons sour cream

PREPARATION

1. Cut the cabbage quarters into fine julienne, crosswise, and toss with the julienned carrot.

2. In the bowl of a food processor or blender, purée the red pepper and (if you're including it) the jalapeño. Add the garlic, vinegar, and ground mustard and celery seed; pulse to purée with the pepper mixture.

3. Add the salt, sugar, and cayenne; with the machine running, slowly drizzle in the oil to emulsify. Add the sour cream and pulse to combine. May be prepared ahead to this point.

4. At least 1 hour before serving, toss the cabbage with the dressing and refrigerate. Check the seasoning and adjust the salt, sugar, and acidity as necessary; serve cool.

Green Corn Pudding

SERVES 8 TO 10

Green corn is an old-fashioned description for fresh corn, to differentiate it from dried corn or, in fact, any but the freshest corn. Despite being called a "pudding," this is, frankly, a casserole—and where would we Southerners be without casseroles? Shame-faced and lost at family reunions and wakes.

This pudding is best served hot out of the oven, but it still eats pretty well at room temperature, or it can be rewarmed in a low oven.

INGREDIENTS

6 ears Silver Queen corn, shucked and silked
4 strips bacon, cut into julienne crosswise
1 cup onion, diced
¾ cup green bell pepper, diced
¾ cup red bell pepper, diced
5 eggs
1 cup heavy cream
¾ cup half-and-half
salt and black pepper to taste
Tabasco and Worcestershire sauce to taste
⅛ teaspoon fresh nutmeg
¼ cup thyme leaves
¼ cup flat-leaf parsley, chopped
1¾ cups grated Vermont white cheddar cheese

PREPARATION

1. Preheat oven to 350°. Cut the kernels off the corn. Using the back of a knife, scrape the "milk" from the cobs. Reserve the corn and "milk."

2. In a sauté pan, cook the bacon over medium heat until crisp. Remove to paper toweling to drain. In the rendered bacon fat, cook the onion and green pepper until soft but not colored. Stir in the red pepper and transfer to a bowl.

3. In a stainless bowl, whisk together the eggs, heavy cream, and half-and-half. Add the cooked vegetables, bacon, and corn. Season with salt, pepper, Tabasco, and Worcestershire sauce. Stir in the nutmeg.

4. Fold in the herbs and cheese and pour the mixture into a buttered 8 × 12-inch ovenproof casserole. Bake for 35 to 40 minutes until set and golden brown. Let rest for 5 minutes before serving.

"Dixie Polenta" (i.e., Creamy Roasted Garlic Grits)

SERVES 8

For those acquainted with congealed, tasteless truck stop grits, we invite you to meet their more voluptuous cousin. These are the real thing: coarsely textured, grainy, with a pure flavor of corn. Augmented by butter, cheese, and light cream, they delight as the base for a wild mushroom ragout, sautéed shrimp, or a stew of shell beans and summer vegetables.

Seek stone-ground white or yellow grits (see Sources), then cook them slowly to achieve that comforting unctuous texture and enjoy!

INGREDIENTS

1 cup coarse, old-fashioned stone-ground grits
1 quart chicken stock
1 tablespoon salt
¼ cup roasted garlic purée (page 245)
4 tablespoons unsalted butter
¼ cup grated Parmesan or Sonoma Dry Jack cheese
¼ cup half-and-half (or more to taste)
salt and black pepper to taste

PREPARATION

1. In a 2- or 3-quart saucepan, heat the chicken stock over high heat until boiling. Add the salt, stir in the grits, and return to a boil. Reduce the heat and simmer 30 to 40 minutes, stirring frequently, until thickened.
2. Stir in the roasted garlic purée, butter, and cheese until incorporated. Stir in the half-and-half and adjust the seasoning. Transfer to a double boiler and keep warm until ready to serve.

Luxe Macaroni & Cheese

SERVES 12 TO 16 AS A SIDE DISH

Sometimes we have to gild the lily. If you prefer, you may substitute other cheeses for the ones specified here. Our son, Gabriel, prefers cheddar, but we still include the ricotta for the creaminess it imparts.

INGREDIENTS

1 pound penne (or other tubular macaroni)
¼ cup unsalted butter
¾ onion, cut into fine dice
¼ cup flour
1 bay leaf
3 cups milk, scalded
salt, black pepper, and nutmeg to taste
1½ cups fontina cheese, grated
2 cups mountain Gorgonzola cheese, crumbled

2 cups mozzarella cheese, cut into ½-inch dice, divided in half

zest of 1 lemon, grated

½ cup fresh basil, chopped

¼ cup Italian parsley, chopped

1 cup whole milk ricotta cheese

1 cup Parmesan cheese, grated, divided in half

½ cup fresh bread crumbs

PREPARATION

1. Preheat oven to 350°.

2. Cook the pasta in boiling, heavily salted water until tender. Drain, transfer to a large bowl, and reserve.

3. In a small saucepan, melt the butter and add the onion, flour, and bay leaf. Cook over low heat, stirring, for 2 minutes. Whisk in the scalded milk, bring to a simmer, and cook over low heat for 10 minutes, whisking frequently, until thickened and smooth. Season liberally with salt, pepper, and nutmeg and strain through a sieve onto the reserved pasta.

4. Add the fontina, the Gorgonzola, half of the mozzarella cubes, the lemon zest, and the herbs. Mix well to combine and transfer half of the pasta to a large shallow casserole or lasagna pan. Sprinkle with the remaining mozzarella cubes, dot with tablespoon portions of the ricotta, and sprinkle with half of the grated Parmesan. Top with the remaining pasta, then sprinkle the surface with bread crumbs and the remaining Parmesan.

5. Bake in a preheated oven for 45 to 50 minutes, until bubbling and GBD (golden brown and delicious). Let rest for 5 minutes and serve.

Carrot-Thyme Spaetzle

SERVES 6 TO 8, DEPENDING ON THE ACCOMPANIMENT

Our spaetzle maker gets a lot of use; we delight in the little dumplings we are able to pair with seafood, game, and poultry dishes. A spaetzle machine resembles a food mill with larger holes in the bottom. If you don't have one, you can press the spaetzle batter through the holes of a colander, using a rubber spatula.

Other vegetable purées work well in place of the carrot purée in this recipe, if you want to try something different. If you find the batter too loose, just stir in flour, a tablespoon at a time, until you achieve the proper consistency.

INGREDIENTS

1¾ cups carrots, peeled and sliced

3 eggs

4 ounces cottage cheese or ricotta cheese

½ teaspoon salt

1 tablespoon fresh thyme leaves

2 cups flour, sifted

clarified butter (page 243) or olive oil for sautéing

1 tablespoon unsalted butter (or to taste)

PREPARATION

1. Put the sliced carrots in an ovenproof dish with 2 tablespoons of water. Cover and bake at 350° for 40 minutes, until tender. Drain well, cool, and purée in a food processor. Reserve.

2. Combine the eggs and cottage cheese in the processor. Add the carrot purée and pulse to combine. Transfer to a bowl.

3. Add the salt and thyme and stir in the flour until combined. Refrigerate, covered, for 30 minutes or more.

4. Put a large pot of water on to boil. Salt generously.

5. Working in batches, pass the batter through a spaetzle machine or colander over the boiling salted water. Cook until puffed and floating. Lift from the water with a slotted spoon or skimmer, cool in an ice water bath, drain well, and toss with oil to coat and prevent sticking. The spaetzle may be prepared ahead to this point and refrigerated.

6. In a nonstick pan, heat oil or butter over medium heat. Sauté the spaetzle in batches until golden. At this point, you may add optional vegetables to the spaetzle, such as greens, root vegetables, or pearl onions. Finish with a knob of butter and serve immediately.

Buttermilk Mashed New Potatoes

SERVES 4 TO 6 AS A SIDE DISH

We love the rustic look of these potatoes, and the wonderful way they feel in your mouth, with their bits of skin and occasional chunks of flesh. The buttermilk adds a delicious tang, but if you can't abide it, you may substitute sour cream for a similar effect. Serve with anything your heart desires.

INGREDIENTS

1½ pounds red-skin new potatoes, unpeeled

¼ pound unsalted butter, cut into pieces, at room temperature

2 tablespoons roasted garlic purée (page 245)

½ cup buttermilk (or more as needed)

salt and black pepper to taste

¼ cup chives, cut into ¼-inch lengths

PREPARATION

1. Wash the potatoes and transfer to a pot, cover with cold water, and add 1 tablespoon salt. Bring to a boil and simmer until the potatoes are tender when pierced with a paring knife.

2. Drain the potatoes, return them to the pot, and place over low heat, covered, for 5 minutes, to steam. Transfer the potatoes to a bowl.

3. With a potato masher or stiff whisk, coarsely mash the potatoes. Beat in the butter to incorporate, then add the roasted garlic purée and buttermilk. Do not overmash; the potatoes should be a little chunky. Season to taste.

4. Rewarm the potatoes over medium heat, stirring with a wooden spoon and adding additional buttermilk if necessary to achieve a creamy texture. Check the seasoning and stir in the chives. Serve immediately.

Molasses Mashed Sweet Potatoes

SERVES 4

Delicately orange and subtly sweet, these mashed potatoes are a great accompaniment to pork, fowl (particularly duck or squab), and game.

INGREDIENTS

½ pound sweet potatoes, peeled and cut into 1-inch rough chunks
½ pound Idaho potatoes, peeled and cut into 1-inch rough chunks
2 tablespoons unsalted butter
2 tablespoons sour cream
2 tablespoons molasses
¼ cup half-and-half, divided
salt and black pepper to taste

PREPARATION

1. Place both the sweet and Idaho potatoes in a saucepan and cover with cold water. Add a pinch of salt and bring to a boil. Simmer until tender, drain, and return to the same saucepan. Place over low heat, cover, and steam for 3 to 5 minutes (to dry out the potatoes).
2. Pass the potatoes through a food mill or potato ricer or mash by hand. Stir in the butter, sour cream, molasses, and 2 tablespoons half-and-half. Season and set aside at room temperature. (May be prepared up to 3 or 4 hours ahead. Cool and cover with plastic film.)
3. In a pan over medium heat, rewarm the potatoes, adding the remaining 2 tablespoons of half-and-half and stirring often, until hot. Check the seasoning. Keep warm until ready to serve.

Sweet Potato & Leek Gratin

SERVES 8 TO 10

Inspired by a recipe from former Grill sous chef Scott Howell, now chef-owner of Nana's in Durham, this gratin is a superb accompaniment to venison or game birds. We find that the gratin slices and portions more readily if made in advance.

INGREDIENTS

1 pound leeks, trimmed, halved lengthwise, sliced crosswise into ¼-inch pieces, and soaked in cold water to cover
2 tablespoons whole unsalted butter
2 tablespoons olive oil
¼ cup garlic, minced
2 cups heavy cream
⅔ cup dried currants or diced pitted prunes
¼ cup fresh thyme
salt and black pepper to taste

1 pound sweet potatoes or garnet yams, peeled

1 ¼ pounds Idaho potatoes, peeled and reserved in cold water

PREPARATION

1. Lift the leeks from the water in which they're soaking so any sand remains in the water. Drain the leeks in a colander. Melt the butter and olive oil in a 2-quart saucepan over medium heat and stir in the leeks and garlic; cover and lower the heat. Cook slowly, stirring occasionally, until the leeks are softened, about 5 minutes. Add the cream, bring to a simmer, and cook over low heat for 5 minutes. Stir in the currants or prunes, fresh thyme, and salt and black pepper to taste. Set aside.

2. Preheat oven to 350°. Butter a heavy-bottomed 5-quart casserole. Using a Japanese mandoline or a sharp knife, slice the sweet potatoes ¼ inch thick. Do the same with the Idaho potatoes. Beginning with Idaho potatoes, arrange a layer of potatoes on the bottom of the casserole. Season lightly with salt and pepper, then spoon 2 tablespoons of leek cream over the potatoes. Repeat with sweet potatoes: layer, season, and spoon leek cream over them. Continue in this way, alternating Idaho and sweet potatoes, until all are used. With your hand, or a rubber spatula, press down firmly on the potatoes; drizzle the remaining leek cream over the top layer. Bake 50 to 60 minutes, until the gratin is bubbling around the edges and a knife slides into it easily. Remove to a warm place and let rest for 15 minutes.

3. Slice the gratin into wedges or squares and serve. It may be prepared ahead and reheated in a 300° oven.

Sweet Potato Salad

SERVES 8 TO 10

Even folks who profess to hate sweet potatoes have admitted liking this salad. Please be sure to return the salad to room temperature if it has been refrigerated and toss it in the dressing once or twice before serving.

INGREDIENTS

2 pounds sweet potatoes, peeled and cut into ½-inch chunks

1 cup pickled pepper relish (page 180), with juices
    (or use commercial relish)

1 teaspoon minced garlic

2 tablespoons Dijon mustard

¼ cup olive oil

salt, black pepper, and Worcestershire sauce

¼ cup Italian parsley, chopped

PREPARATION

1. Cook the sweet potatoes in salted water until done but still firm. Plunge them in ice water to stop them from cooking and drain well.

2. Combine the relish, garlic, and Dijon mustard in a bowl. Whisk in the olive oil, as well as salt, pepper, and Worcestershire sauce to taste.
3. Fold in the sweet potatoes and Italian parsley and toss gently. Keeps refrigerated for 2 days.
4. Serve at room temperature.

Crawfish Jambalaya Risotto

SERVES 6 TO 8

Deep, rounded Cajun flavors combined with a bit of Italian technique result in this rather substantial side dish that is definitely not afraid. While terrific paired with grilled pork or game birds, this preparation can also be bulked up with some braised rabbit or poached chicken (stirred in at the end) and make a very satisfying entrée on its own.

INGREDIENTS

2 ounces peanut oil
4 ounces andouille sausage, cut into quarters lengthwise and sliced thin crosswise
1 cup onion, cut into small dice
⅔ cup celery, cut into small dice
½ cup green bell pepper, cut into small dice
½ cup red bell pepper, cut into small dice
2 tablespoons garlic, minced
2 cups Arborio rice
½ teaspoon cayenne pepper
1 teaspoon paprika
1 cup canned tomatoes, seeded and chopped
1 cup white wine
5 cups chicken stock (or crawfish stock; see note)
½ pound crawfish tail meat (or 31–35 count shrimp, peeled)
2 tablespoons fresh sage leaves, cut into chiffonade
2 tablespoons parsley, chopped
3 tablespoons unsalted butter
¼ cup grated Parmesan cheese
salt and black pepper to taste

PREPARATION

1. In a straight-sided, heavy-bottomed saucepan, heat the oil over medium heat. Add the sausage and cook until lightly browned. Remove the sausage and set aside. Add the onion, celery, and green and red peppers to the oil remaining in the pan and cook over medium heat until softened and lightly colored. Add the garlic and rice and cook 2 minutes, until the rice becomes opalescent. Add the cayenne and paprika.
2. Stir in the tomatoes and wine, bring to a boil, and cook, stirring, until the liquid is absorbed. Add 1 cup chicken stock and cook, stirring, until the liquid is absorbed. Continue adding stock in 1-cup increments (it usually takes a total

of 4 cups) until the rice is creamy but still firm in the center. Spread the rice on a sheet pan or cookie sheet to cool. (May be prepared ahead to this point.)

3. Finish the risotto. In a heavy-bottomed saucepan, combine the cooled risotto and 1 cup chicken stock. Heat over medium-high heat, stirring, until the rice thickens. Check for doneness, adding more stock if necessary. Stir in the crawfish tail meat, sausage, herbs, butter, and cheese; adjust the seasoning.

Note: If you are cooking your own crawfish, reserve the shells and simmer in chicken stock for 15 minutes. Strain and reserve, substituting for straight chicken stock in the recipe.

Wild Mushroom Bread Pudding

SERVES 12

When a customer came back from New Orleans raving about the wild mushroom bread pudding she had eaten at Emeril's, we wanted to try to replicate it for her birthday. This recipe owes its inspiration to everything Emeril Lagasse cooks: it's full-throttle and complex with deep flavors. It makes a wonderful, albeit rich, side dish to accompany roasted poultry or grilled rabbit; you may want to consider it as a vegetarian entrée with a salad or a ragout of seasonal vegetables.

INGREDIENTS

2 1-pound day-old baguettes, crusts trimmed, cut into 1-inch cubes
    and left to dry out for 1 to 2 hours
4 cups half-and-half
4 cups heavy cream
1 ½ ounces dried porcini mushrooms
1 bay leaf
2 tablespoons clarified butter (page 243)
12 ounces assorted wild mushrooms, sliced
1 shallot, minced
6 eggs
4 egg yolks
¼ cup roasted garlic purée (page 245)
2 tablespoons fresh thyme, chopped
½ teaspoon Worcestershire sauce
½ teaspoon Tabasco
salt, black pepper, and freshly grated nutmeg to taste
3 tablespoons grated Parmesan cheese

PREPARATION

1. In a stainless saucepot, combine the half-and-half, heavy cream, porcini mushrooms, and bay leaf. Bring to a simmer, remove from heat, cover, and allow to steep 30 minutes.

2. Over high heat, sauté the wild mushrooms in clarified butter; when the

mushrooms are cooked through, add the minced shallot to the pan, toss to combine, remove from heat, and reserve.

3. In a large bowl, combine the eggs, egg yolks, roasted garlic purée, fresh thyme, Worcestershire sauce, Tabasco, salt, pepper, and freshly grated nutmeg. The mixture should be assertively seasoned.

4. Strain the cream into the egg mixture, whisking to combine. Discard the bay leaf and mince the porcini mushrooms. Add these to the egg mixture along with the cooked wild mushrooms. Fold in the bread cubes, toss to combine, and allow to soak for 15 minutes. Meanwhile, preheat oven to 350°.

5. Place the mixture in a buttered 12-cup shallow casserole and sprinkle with Parmesan cheese. Place the casserole in a water bath. Bake, uncovered, for approximately 40 to 45 minutes, until the top is crusty and the custard is set. (This can be made up to 2 days ahead. Reheat thoroughly before serving.)

Carolina Grits Soufflé

SERVES 8

This wonderful side dish is inspired by a recipe from Ben's mama, fancied up a bit. It's cheeze-a-licious!

INGREDIENTS

2 cups homemade chicken stock + 1 cup water (or use 3 cups water instead)
1 cup half-and-half
2 teaspoons salt
1 cup white grits, preferably stone-ground, definitely not instant
5 eggs, separated
1 ½ cups white or yellow sharp cheddar, grated
¼ cup roasted garlic purée (page 245) or 1 tablespoon minced fresh garlic
4 tablespoons unsalted butter
salt, coarsely ground black pepper, and Tabasco to taste
½ cup scallions, sliced thin crosswise

PREPARATION

1. Butter a 2-quart casserole or soufflé dish.

2. In a 3-quart, heavy-bottomed saucepan, bring the stock, water, half-and-half, and salt to a boil. Stir in the grits, reduce the heat to medium, and cook, stirring often, until thick, smooth, and creamy (the consistency of polenta).

3. Beat the egg yolks, temper with a spoonful of hot grits, and then stir into the grits. Stir in the cheese, garlic purée, and butter, and season with salt, pepper, and Tabasco to taste. Cool at room temperature.

4. An hour before serving, preheat oven to 375°. In a stainless steel bowl, beat the egg whites until they form stiff peaks. Gently fold the egg whites and scallions into the grits mixture and spoon into the buttered soufflé dish. Bake 30 to 40 minutes, until the grits are set. (If the surface appears to be browning too much, cover with foil until set.) Serve immediately.

Spoonbread

MAKES 12 TO 14 PORTIONS

This is a lighter version of traditional spoonbread; by separating the eggs and beating the egg whites, a soufflé effect is achieved—but there's certainly no compromise in flavor. You can let your imagination run wild as far as creating flavor combinations goes. Our friend Damon Lee Fowler, author of *Classical Southern Cooking* and *Beans, Greens and Sweet Georgia Peaches*, particularly likes a variant with leeks and Roquefort.

For the best results, your cooked base and egg whites should be at room temperature before beating the whites.

INGREDIENTS FOR THE BASE

2½ cups milk

2 cups half-and-half

1 tablespoon salt

1 tablespoon sugar

1 cup cornmeal

½ cup flour

8 tablespoons unsalted butter, cut into pieces

6 eggs, separated

¼ cup heavy cream

FLAVORING OPTIONS

¾ cup of any of the following can be added to the base before folding in the egg whites:

quince or apple purée

sweet potato, butternut, or winter squash purée

Vidalia onion or leek purée

cooked bacon or country ham

chopped herbs, the kitchen sink, etc.

PREPARATION

1. Lightly butter a 12-cup shallow casserole.
2. Heat the milk, half-and-half, salt, and sugar in a heavy saucepan over medium heat. When small bubbles appear around the edge, slowly whisk in the cornmeal and flour, stirring constantly. Continue to stir as the mixture cooks and thickens. When smooth and creamy, remove from heat and stir in the butter until completely absorbed.
3. Beat the egg yolks and cream together until lightened in color. Gradually add to the cornmeal mixture. Next, add the flavoring option of your choice. Season generously before folding in the egg whites. The base can be made ahead to this point.
4. Preheat oven to 350°. Beat the egg whites. Fold into the cornmeal mixture. Spread in the buttered casserole. Bake until puffy, golden brown, and just set, about 30 to 35 minutes. Serve immediately.

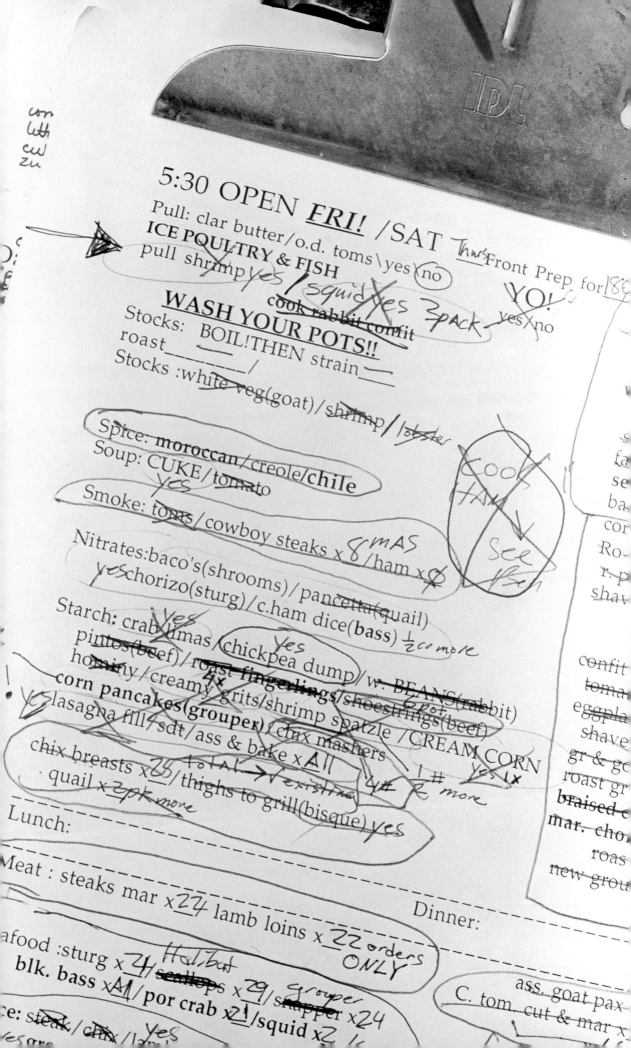

Squash Casserole

SERVES 8 TO 10

Every Southern family has its own recipe for simple, down-home squash casserole. This version is based on a recipe from Ben's mother. It is just as delicious served at room temperature as it is hot, and it may be prepared in advance and reheated.

INGREDIENTS

 3 tablespoons rendered bacon fat

 1 large onion, peeled and cut into small dice

 3 pounds yellow squash, cut lengthwise into quarters
  and sliced ¼ inch thick

¼ cup water

 1 cup grated Monterey Jack cheese

 ½ cup grated Parmesan cheese

3 tablespoons chopped parsley

3 tablespoons chopped sage

4 eggs, beaten

salt, freshly ground black pepper, and Tabasco to taste

PREPARATION

1. Preheat oven to 350°.

2. Heat the bacon fat in a large skillet over medium heat. Add the onion and cook till softened. Add the squash and sauté 5 minutes. Add the water and steam, covered, until tender.

3. Strain the squash mixture, discarding the liquid, and place the squash in a mixing bowl. Combine with the Jack cheese, Parmesan, parsley, sage, and eggs. Mix well and season to taste with salt, black pepper, and Tabasco.

4. Pour the mixture into a greased shallow 12-cup casserole.

5. Bake approximately 30 to 35 minutes, until set and golden brown.

Bean's Black Skillet Cornbread

MAKES 1 8-INCH CAST-IRON SKILLET'S WORTH

Yankee cornbread tends to be cakey and sweet. For years we've tried to duplicate Ben's notion of what perfect Southern-style cornbread should be. After much consultation with his mom (whose nickname is Bean, by the way), we developed this recipe. A coarse-ground cornmeal is needed to attain the proper crumbly texture, buttermilk supplies the tang, and bacon fat, while not mandatory, is traditional.

INGREDIENTS

    1 cup stone-ground yellow cornmeal
    ¾ teaspoon salt
    1 teaspoon sugar
    ⅛ teaspoon baking soda
    1½ teaspoons baking powder
    2 eggs
    1 cup buttermilk
    2 tablespoons melted butter
    1 tablespoon rendered melted bacon fat + 1 tablespoon rendered melted
      bacon fat for greasing the skillet

PREPARATION

    1. Preheat oven to 450°. Place an 8-inch cast-iron skillet in the oven.
    2. Combine the cornmeal, salt, sugar, baking soda, and baking powder in a large
       bowl. Reserve.
    3. In a separate bowl, beat the eggs with the buttermilk till smooth. Add the
       melted butter and 1 tablespoon bacon fat. Mix the liquid ingredients into the
       dry ingredients.
    4. Carefully remove the hot skillet from the oven and coat with 1 tablespoon of
       bacon fat. Pour the batter into the skillet, place the skillet on the top oven rack,
       and bake approximately 15 to 20 minutes, until the cornbread is set and lightly
       browned, and starts to pull away from the sides of the pan. Allow to cool
       slightly. It is best served warm.

Note: You can double this recipe and bake it in a 10-inch skillet if desired. If you do not own a cast-iron skillet, you can bake this cornbread in a traditional baking pan. We strongly urge you, however, to keep a few cast-iron pieces in your kitchen battery. They are inexpensive, multipurpose, and invaluable for certain cooking tasks.

Buttermilk Bread

This simple bread makes a great sandwich loaf and is really good toasted or pan griddled. We use it for our fried green tomato sandwich (page 144), but it also lends itself to being paired with fresh sliced tomatoes and pimiento cheese.

INGREDIENTS

- 1 tablespoon granulated yeast
- ¼ cup warm water
- 1 tablespoon sugar
- ¾ cup buttermilk
- 1 tablespoon unsalted butter, at room temperature
- 1 egg
- 3 cups all-purpose flour
- ¼ teaspoon baking soda
- 1 teaspoon salt

PREPARATION

1. Dissolve the yeast in the warm water and allow to proof.
2. Stir in the sugar, buttermilk, and butter.
3. Stir in the egg.
4. Add 2 cups of flour, the baking soda, and the salt to the above mixture. Add enough additional flour to form a smooth and soft, but not sticky, dough. It should take approximately 1 more cup, but you might need a bit more or less. Knead approximately 10 minutes. Place the dough in a lightly greased bowl, cover, and let rise until doubled.
5. Shape the dough into a loaf and place it in a greased 6-cup loaf pan. Let rise until almost doubled.
6. Preheat oven to 350°. Bake for approximately 45 to 50 minutes, until the top crust is nicely browned and the bread tests done. When turned out of the pan, the bread should be golden brown on the bottom and sound hollow when tapped. Turn out onto a rack and cool completely.

Buttermilk Herb Crackers

MAKES APPROXIMATELY 60 CRACKERS

This easy cracker recipe is really a biscuit dough made with half as much buttermilk as you would normally use. The crackers will keep well for several days if stored in an airtight container.

INGREDIENTS

    2 cups White Lily self-rising flour
    2 ounces shortening, chilled and cut into pieces
    2 tablespoons finely snipped chives
    approximately ⅓–½ cup cold buttermilk

PREPARATION

1. In a food processor with a steel blade, cut the cold shortening into the flour, using a pulse motion, till the mixture resembles coarse meal. Pulse in the chives.
2. Gradually pulse in approximately ⅓ to ½ cup buttermilk. The dough should just come together and should be pliable but not at all sticky.
3. Divide the dough into quarters and flatten each into a disc. Working with each disc individually, run the dough through a pasta machine, flouring occasionally, until the dough is very thin (approximately 1 to 1½ on the roller settings, or ¹⁄₁₆ inch thick). Alternatively, you can roll the discs out by hand, using a lightly floured rolling pin.
4. Cut 2 × 2 × 3-inch triangles out of the thinly rolled dough and place them on a parchment-lined baking sheet. Pierce each cracker once or twice with a fork. Bake at 350° till golden brown.
5. Cool completely and store in an airtight container.

Hushpuppies

YIELDS 30 TO 35

Traditional in barbecue restaurants and fish camps since time immemorial, these are a fine accompaniment to a Southern vegetable supper, and they may also be served as an hors d'oeuvre with smoked tomato remoulade (page 69) or as a garnish for schoolkids' flounder with fish camp beurre blanc (page 137).

INGREDIENTS

    3½ cups stone-ground cornmeal
    1½ cups all-purpose flour
    1 tablespoon + 1 teaspoon baking powder
    2 teaspoons baking soda
    2 teaspoons salt
    ½ teaspoon cayenne pepper
    ⅔ cup onion, finely chopped
    ½ cup green bell pepper, finely chopped

2 jalapeños, red or green, seeded and minced (or more to taste)
4 eggs
2 ¼ cups buttermilk
½ cup green onions, chopped
peanut oil for frying

PREPARATION

1. In a large bowl, combine the cornmeal, flour, baking powder, baking soda, salt, and cayenne. Stir to mix well. Add the onion, green pepper, and jalapeños; stir to blend.
2. In a bowl, whisk together the eggs and buttermilk. Fold into the dry mixture. Check the seasoning. If the mixture seems dry, add a little more buttermilk. Fold in the green onions.
3. In a deep-fryer or heavy pot, heat peanut oil to 360° (use a deep-frying thermometer). Using a 1-ounce scoop or a large spoon, drop spoonfuls of batter into the hot oil, 6 to 8 at a time, and fry until deep golden brown.
4. Drain on a paper bag and keep warm in a low oven while frying the remainder of the hushpuppies. Serve immediately.

Angel Biscuits

YIELDS 3 DOZEN

Triple risen with yeast, baking powder, and soda, angel biscuits, also known as bride's biscuits, are virtually foolproof in nature—even novice bakers can turn out light and flaky biscuits using this recipe.

INGREDIENTS

- ¾ tablespoon yeast
- 2 tablespoons warm water
- 3¾ cups all-purpose flour
- ¾ tablespoon baking powder
- 1 teaspoon baking soda
- 3 tablespoons sugar
- ¾ tablespoon salt
- ½ cup vegetable shortening, at room temperature
- 1½ cups buttermilk

PREPARATION

1. In a small bowl, dissolve the yeast in the warm water with a small pinch of sugar.
2. Place the flour, baking powder, baking soda, sugar, and salt in a mixing bowl. Cut in the shortening till evenly distributed. Add the buttermilk and the yeast mixture and mix till evenly moistened. This can be done with a stationary mixer if desired.
3. Place the dough in a greased storage container, cover, and refrigerate 8 to 36 hours.
4. Turn the dough out onto a lightly floured surface and roll out about ½ inch thick. Cut with a 2-inch biscuit cutter and place the biscuits 1 inch apart on a parchment-lined or lightly greased baking sheet. Allow to rise at room temperature approximately 1 hour, till puffy. Toward the end of the hour, preheat the oven to 375°.
5. Bake 15 to 20 minutes, till lightly browned. These can be baked several hours ahead if desired. Store covered at room temperature; reheat before serving if desired.

Abundance Plum Chutney

YIELDS 7 CUPS

Sweet and yet piquant, this chutney is made from an heirloom variety of plum known for—and taking its name from—its prolific production. Substitutes would be Japanese-type yellow plums, greengages, or lighter-skinned, orange-fleshed varieties. Serve with smoked or grilled meats and poultry.

INGREDIENTS

    2 cups onion, finely diced

    2 tablespoons peanut or safflower oil

    1 teaspoon curry spice blend (page 244) or commercial curry spice

    ½ cup white sugar

    ½ cup brown sugar

    1 cup cider vinegar

    2 teaspoons salt

    ½ teaspoon allspice

    1 teaspoon freshly ground white pepper

    3 pounds Abundance or greengage plums, slightly underripe,
        pitted and cut into fourths or eighths, depending on size

    ½ cup dried cranberries or cherries

PREPARATION

    1. Cook the onion in the oil until soft but not colored.

    2. Add the curry spice and cook 1 minute.

    3. Add the sugars, vinegar, salt, allspice, and white pepper and bring to a simmer.

    4. Add the plums and dried fruit. Simmer until the fruit is done but still firm.

    5. Adjust the acidity with more vinegar, or the sweetness with a dollop of
       molasses. Keeps 2 weeks, refrigerated.

Green Tomato Butter

YIELDS APPROXIMATELY 6 CUPS

This is like apple butter, but tangy, with a funky pale green color. Since this recipe will give you a larger quantity of tomato butter than you'll need for most applications, use the extra as a sandwich spread or condiment. It keeps indefinitely, refrigerated.

INGREDIENTS

    ½ cup cider vinegar

    ½ cup brown sugar

    ½ cup white sugar

    1 teaspoon salt

    sachet bag containing 1 cinnamon stick, broken; 3 whole cloves, cracked;
       and 3 allspice berries, crushed

    2½ pounds green tomatoes, peeled and cored

    8 ounces Vidalia onions, minced

PREPARATION

    1. Combine the vinegar, sugars, salt, and spice bag in a heavy pan; bring to a boil.

    2. Add the tomatoes and onions and simmer over low heat until thick, stirring
       often.

    3. Cool, then purée in a food processor. Refrigerate.

Piccalilli

Sweet and tart at the same time, this tangy relish made with green tomatoes is a treat we don't wait for autumn's first frost to make. Just request firm tomatoes from your grower or pick those candidates that you know won't ripen before the end of the growing season.

The volume of liquid in the initial cooking may seem small, but the vegetables release their juices as they cook.

Serve with soups or vegetable salads or as a condiment for smoked or cured seafood.

INGREDIENTS

  3 pounds medium green tomatoes, cut into small dice (¼ inch)
  1 cup chopped onion
  3 green bell peppers, seeded, demembraned, and cut into small dice
  3 red bell peppers, seeded, demembraned, and cut into small dice
  1 ½ yellow bell peppers, seeded, demembraned, and cut into small dice
  3 cups cider vinegar, divided
  1 ¾ cups sugar
  2 tablespoons salt
  1 teaspoon allspice berries, ground
  2 cinnamon sticks
  1 tablespoon celery seed
  ¼ cup mustard seed
  1 spray fresh bay leaves (optional)

PREPARATION

  1. Wash the vegetables and cut up as specified.
  2. Place the vegetables in a 4-quart nonreactive Dutch oven or kettle. Add 2 cups vinegar and bring to a boil. Boil for 30 minutes, uncovered, stirring frequently. Drain and discard the liquid.
  3. Return the vegetables to the kettle. Add the remaining cup of vinegar and the sugar, salt, and spices. (Add the spray of fresh bay leaves, if using.) Bring to a boil and simmer 3 minutes.
  4. If you are canning the piccalilli, remove the bay leaves and cinnamon sticks, follow standard procedure, and process for 15 minutes. Or you can store it in sterilized glass jars (refrigerated) for up to 6 months in lieu of canning.

Note: This recipe can easily be doubled if you wish to give a jar of piccalilli to all your friends.

Iowa Corn Relish

YIELDS ABOUT 2 QUARTS

One of our great line cooks, an Iowa native known affectionately as "Homer" or "Corn-fed," declared this recipe was good enough to come from his home state—thus the name. Wherever it comes from, it makes a fine table condiment, foundation for a vinaigrette, or finish-in-a-pan sauce. It keeps indefinitely refrigerated, or you may can it in the traditional fashion.

INGREDIENTS

10 ears sweet corn (about 5 cups cut off cob)
½ cup green bell pepper, cut into small dice
½ cup red bell pepper, cut into small dice
½ cup red onion, cut into small dice
½ cup yellow onion, cut into small dice
½ cup celery, cut into small dice
¾ cup sugar
1 ½ teaspoons mustard seed
½ teaspoon celery seed
¼ teaspoon ground turmeric
2 cups cider vinegar
1 ½ cups water
12 whole cloves garlic
4 whole dried chipotles

PREPARATION

1. Husk the corn and cut the kernels off the cob.
2. Combine all of the ingredients, except the corn, in a 3-quart stainless pot. Simmer for 15 minutes, add the corn kernels, and continue to simmer for 5 more minutes.
3. Cool and store in *clean* glass jars. Refrigerate.

Pickled Pepper Relish

YIELDS 2 PINTS

Sweet pepper relish constantly finds its way into vinaigrettes and mayonnaises at the restaurant. It has a zesty sweetness that complements roasted or grilled pork and is particularly attractive with smoked poultry.

INGREDIENTS

1 cup green bell pepper, seeded, stemmed, and cut into small dice

1 ½ cups red bell pepper, seeded, stemmed, and cut into small dice

¾ cup red onion, cut into small dice (1 medium onion)

boiling water

6 ounces cider vinegar

3 ounces sugar

1 ½ teaspoons salt

½ teaspoon celery seed

2 dried chipotles, halved and seeded (optional)

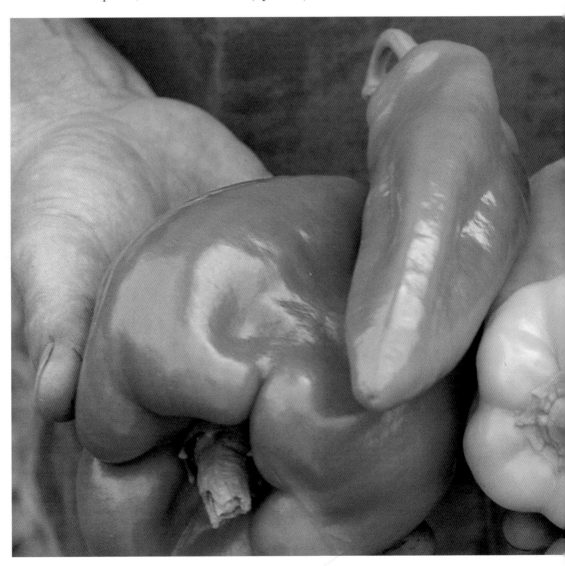

1. Place the vegetables in a 2-quart nonreactive pot. Pour in enough boiling water to cover the vegetables and let stand for 10 minutes. Drain.

2. Add the vinegar, salt, sugar, celery seed, and (optional) chipotles to the vegetables. Bring to a boil and then simmer over low heat for 15 minutes.

3. Ladle into 2 hot pint jars and fill to within ¼ inch of the rim. Wipe the rim, seal the lids, and process in a boiling water bath for 15 minutes. Start timing *after* the water bath reaches full boil.

4. Check to be sure the jars are securely sealed. The relish will keep for up to 6 months.

5. In lieu of being canned, this relish can be refrigerated for up to 3 months, covered, in clean, sterile containers.

6. This recipe can be scaled up easily, but be cautious with the chipotles.

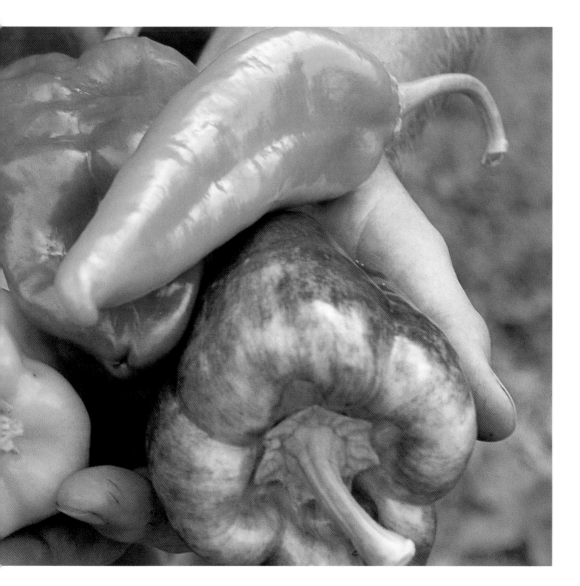

desserts

The Chef's Favorite Lemon Tart

Chocolate Peanut Praline Tart

Walnut Sun-Dried Cranberry Tart
with Cranberry & Orange Compote

Brown Sugar Pear Poundcake

Banana Pecan Crostata

Blueberry-Peach (or Nectarine) Pie

Deep-Dish Apple Cinnamon Crisp
with Brandied Vanilla Ice Cream

Maple View Dairy Buttermilk Cheesecake

Chocolate-Raspberry Soufflé Cake

Ginger-Lime Crème Caramels
with Tropical Ambrosia

Double Chocolate Waffles with Strawberries
& White Chocolate Ice Cream

Jack Daniels Vanilla Ice Cream

Peach Ice Cream

White Chocolate Ice Cream

Watermelon Granita

Concord Grape Sorbet

White Grape Jello

Old-Fashioned Peanut Butter Cookies

Sugar Magnolias: Karen's Guide to Sweet Endings

Although I went through the general program at the Culinary Institute of America, creating sweet stuff has always been my primary focus. Following the same principles as those used in savory cooking, I aim for an optimum amount of sweetness in any given dessert, balanced with texture and temperature contrasts. A great deal of emphasis is placed on the dessert course at Magnolia Grill, where the baking style can best be described as down-home American with a twist. While I admire the artistry entailed in the architectural school of dessert making, my baking tends to be straightforward and focuses on flavor.

Our desserts are built from a series of components. They often feature a base item—such as a tart, poundcake, particular type of poached fruit, etc.—to which we add a sauce, an ice cream, or perhaps a cookie garnish. These individual recipes are prepared ahead of time and then combined for the final dessert presentation.

Do try new ideas of your own, using these recipes as a guideline, but remember to pay attention to how something looks, smells, and feels. Learn to trust your senses. This is particularly important in the case of baking times. My rule of thumb is to start checking for doneness 5 to 10 minutes *before* the recipe specifies. I have tried to include visual clues in the recipes to help you determine when something is properly baked. If the item has not finished baking but seems "close," check it every few minutes thereafter.

If you look at the collection of recipes given in this section as building blocks, you can adapt them to suit any time restrictions you might have. Most pastry and cookie doughs can be made ahead and frozen if they're well wrapped and then allowed to defrost overnight in your refrigerator before use. Sauces and compotes will also keep well for several days, and, again, many can be frozen. If you don't have the time, inclination, or equipment to make one of the accompanying ice cream garnishes, you can substitute a premium store-bought ice cream. I have included a section on impromptu dessert ideas that can be realized from base recipes (some provided in this section and some being standards, like brownies or shortcake, that can easily be found elsewhere) and turned into very different desserts by varying their treatment. I encourage you to experiment, adapt, and, most of all, have fun!

The Chef's Favorite Lemon Tart

MAKES 1 10½-INCH TART; SERVES 8 TO 12

The chef's favorite lemon tart is a somewhat sophisticated take on Southern-style lemon chess pie. This simple tart really is one of Ben's favorite desserts and has been a standard in Karen's repertoire for close to 20 years.

We most often serve this with a mixture of seasonal berries and lightly whipped cream. You can substitute a simple raspberry sauce made from frozen raspberries if it is not fresh berry season.

INGREDIENTS FOR THE TART SHELL

- 1¼ cups + 2 tablespoons flour
- 1 tablespoon + 1 teaspoon sugar
- ⅛ teaspoon salt
- 8 tablespoons cold unsalted butter, cut into small pieces
- 1 large egg yolk, beaten with 1 tablespoon milk
- 1 egg white, lightly beaten, reserved for baking

INGREDIENTS FOR THE FILLING

- 4 eggs
- 1½ cups sugar
- ½ cup orange juice
- ½ cup lemon juice
- zest of 1 lemon, grated
- zest of 1 orange, grated
- ¼ cup heavy cream

INGREDIENTS FOR SERVICE

- fresh berries (or berry sauce [page 220])
- whipped cream (page 221)

PREPARATION FOR THE TART SHELL

1. In a food processor, pulse together the flour, sugar, and salt. Add the butter and pulse until the mixture resembles coarse meal. Add the egg yolk mixture and pulse just until the dough can be gathered into a ball. Flatten into a 6-inch disc, wrap in plastic, and chill several hours or overnight. Let the dough soften slightly at room temperature before rolling.

2. On a lightly floured surface, roll the dough into a 13-inch round. Fit the dough into a 10½-inch tart pan with a removable bottom. Trim the dough flush with the rim and freeze the tart shell until firm. Meanwhile, preheat oven to 350°.

3. Line the shell with foil or parchment, and fill with pie weights, rice, or dried beans. Bake for 20 minutes until set. Remove the foil and weights and bake an additional 10 to 15 minutes until lightly golden. Remove the shell from the oven and immediately brush the hot pastry with the egg white.

Hint: When rolling tart pastry, always save all the dough scraps in case you need them to repair a crack in a partially baked shell. If the pastry "bubbles up" during the baking process, gently prick the pastry with a fork to release air bubbles. Check several times and repeat if necessary. The egg white serves to seal the pastry, which is especially helpful with a liquid filling such as this. It is essential that there be no cracks or holes visible in the partially baked shell. Make any necessary repairs prior to filling.

PREPARATION FOR THE TART

1. When the pastry is almost done baking, assemble the filling. Whisk together the eggs, sugar, orange juice, lemon juice, lemon zest, and orange zest and cream till smooth. Transfer the tart shell to the oven. Place the filling in a pitcher and slowly pour into the shell as high as possible without overfilling. There might be a bit of filling left over.

2. Bake the tart for approximately 25 minutes, until the filling is barely set. Check the tart after 20 minutes and keep checking it every few minutes after that. It is crucial to not overbake this filling!

3. Cool to room temperature before serving with berries and whipped cream.

Chocolate Peanut Praline Tart

MAKES 1 10½-INCH TART, OR 10 TO 12 PORTIONS

This ultrarich confection is a real crowd-pleaser. It makes a wonderful addition to a dessert buffet or sampler because a small slice really does go a long way. Those with a penchant for candy bars will, however, want their own full-size piece . . . with whipped cream.

INGREDIENTS FOR THE TART SHELL

1¼ cups + 2 tablespoons flour

1 tablespoon + 1 teaspoon sugar

⅛ teaspoon salt

8 tablespoons cold unsalted butter, cut into small pieces

1 large egg yolk, beaten with 1 tablespoon milk

1 egg white, lightly beaten, reserved for baking

INGREDIENTS FOR THE CHOCOLATE FILLING

5½ ounces semisweet chocolate

7 tablespoons unsalted butter

2 eggs

¼ cup sugar

2 tablespoons flour

3 tablespoons bourbon

INGREDIENTS FOR THE PRALINE TOPPING

1½ cups unsalted peanuts, lightly toasted and chopped

8 tablespoons unsalted butter

6 tablespoons brown sugar

3 tablespoons sugar

½ cup heavy cream

½ teaspoon vanilla extract

INGREDIENT FOR SERVING

whipped cream (page 221)

PREPARATION

1. To make the tart shell: In a food processor pulse together the flour, sugar, and salt. Add the butter and pulse until the mixture resembles coarse meal. Add the egg yolk mixture and pulse just until the dough can be gathered into a ball. Flatten into a 6-inch disc, wrap in plastic, and chill for several hours or overnight. Let the dough soften slightly at room temperature before rolling.

2. On a lightly floured surface, roll the dough into a 13-inch round. Fit the dough into a 10½-inch tart pan with a removable bottom. Trim the dough flush with the rim and freeze the tart shell till firm. Meanwhile, preheat oven to 350°.

3. Line the shell with foil or parchment and fill with pie weights, rice, or dried beans. Bake for 20 minutes until set. Remove the parchment and weights and bake an additional 10 to 15 minutes, until lightly golden. Immediately brush the hot pastry with the reserved egg white.

4. While the pastry is baking, assemble the filling. Melt the semisweet chocolate and butter in a double boiler and reserve.

5. Whisk the eggs with the sugar and flour. Whisk in the bourbon, and then whisk in the melted chocolate–butter mixture. Pour the filling into the prepared tart shell. Bake until the filling is just barely set, approximately 10 to 12 minutes, then remove from the oven. Scatter the toasted, chopped peanuts evenly over the tart surface.

6. For the praline topping, melt the butter in a small saucepan. Add the brown and white sugars and simmer over medium heat for 5 minutes. Add the cream and vanilla and simmer the mixture for an additional 5 to 8 minutes, until thickened. Immediately spoon the praline topping evenly over the peanuts to lightly cover the surface of the tart. You may not need all the praline topping— do not overfill.

7. Place the tart in the refrigerator to set the topping (approximately 2 hours). Serve at room temperature with whipped cream.

Note: This tart can be made up to 48 hours ahead of time. Wrap it lightly *once the topping is set* or keep it under a dome if prepared in advance.

Walnut Sun-Dried Cranberry Tart with Cranberry & Orange Compote

MAKES 1 10½-INCH TART; SERVES 10

This chewy, crunchy, and totally delicious tart is a perfect addition to the holiday season dessert repertoire. While you can serve it simply, with just the accompanying fruit compote, most guests wouldn't mind an added embellishment of whipped cream or vanilla ice cream.

INGREDIENTS FOR THE TART SHELL

> 1¼ cups + 2 tablespoons flour
> 1 tablespoon + 1 teaspoon sugar
> ⅛ teaspoon salt
> 8 tablespoons cold unsalted butter, cut into small pieces
> 1 large egg yolk, beaten with 1 tablespoon milk
> 1 egg white, lightly beaten, reserved for baking

INGREDIENTS FOR THE FILLING

> 4 eggs
> ½ cup sugar
> 1 tablespoon flour
> ⅛ teaspoon salt
> 1 teaspoon vanilla extract
> zest of 2 oranges, grated
> 1 cup light corn syrup
> 1 tablespoon orange juice concentrate, thawed
> 2 tablespoons Grand Marnier
> 8 tablespoons unsalted butter, melted
> 8 ounces sun-dried cranberries
> 1½ cups walnut pieces, lightly toasted, skins removed, and chopped

INGREDIENTS FOR THE COMPOTE

> 1½ cups fresh cranberries
> ½ cup sugar
> ¼ cup orange juice
> 4 navel oranges, peeled and cut into segments
> 1 tablespoon Grand Marnier

OPTIONAL FOR SERVICE

> whipped cream (page 221) or vanilla ice cream

PREPARATION FOR THE TART SHELL

> 1. In a food processor, pulse together the flour, sugar, and salt. Add the butter and pulse until the mixture resembles coarse meal. Add the egg yolk mixture and pulse just until the dough can be gathered into a ball. Flatten into a 6-inch disc, wrap in plastic, and chill several hours or overnight. Let the dough soften slightly at room temperature before rolling.

2. On a lightly floured surface, roll the dough into a 13-inch round. Fit the dough into a 10½-inch tart pan with a removable bottom. Trim the dough flush with the rim and freeze the shell until firm. Meanwhile, preheat oven to 350°.

3. Line the shell with parchment or foil and fill with pie weights, rice, or beans. Bake for 20 minutes until set. Remove the foil and weights and bake an additional 10 to 15 minutes until lightly golden. Immediately brush the hot pastry with the egg white.

PREPARATION FOR THE TART

1. When the pastry is almost done baking, assemble the filling. Whisk together all the filling ingredients and pour into the prepared, partially baked shell.

2. Bake for approximately 45 minutes, until the filling is puffed, set, and lightly browned. Transfer the tart to a cooling rack and allow to come to room temperature. The tart can be made up to 24 hours ahead. Store covered at room temperature. Serve with cranberry and orange compote and with whipped cream or ice cream if desired.

PREPARATION FOR THE COMPOTE

1. In a small skillet, combine the cranberries with the orange juice and sugar. Cook over low heat, stirring often, just until the cranberries pop and soften, about 4 minutes. Remove from the heat.

2. Add the oranges and stir in the Grand Marnier. Taste and adjust the sugar if necessary. Cool the mixture over an ice bath, stirring occasionally. Store covered in the refrigerator if not using right away.

Brown Sugar Pear Poundcake

FILLS 1 10-INCH BUNDT PAN; SERVES 14 TO 16

There is something innately satisfying and "homey" about a slice of good poundcake. Our dessert menu changes with the seasons, and we often feature a generous wedge of lightly toasted poundcake topped with ice cream and accompanied by a fresh seasonal fruit sauce. In the case of this pear-accented variation, we think pear sauce, a scoop of vanilla bean ice cream, and a drizzle of butterscotch sauce turn the simple into something sublime.

This recipe evolved from Maida Heatter's Kentucky poundcake recipe that was first published in her *Book of Great Desserts*. Heatter is truly a dessert goddess, and we would heartily endorse the idea of buying her complete collection of cookbooks, which are jam-packed with wonderful creations.

INGREDIENTS FOR THE CAKE

    3½ cups flour
    1½ teaspoons baking powder
    ½ teaspoon salt
    24 tablespoons unsalted butter (3 sticks), at room temperature
    zest of 1 orange, grated

1 tablespoon vanilla extract

3 cups light brown sugar

5 eggs

¾ cup milk

¼ cup pear brandy, plain brandy, or orange juice

2¼ cups ripe but firm pears, peeled and cut into ¼-inch dice

INGREDIENTS FOR THE GLAZE

⅓ cup sugar

⅓ cup pear brandy, plain brandy, or orange juice

OPTIONAL INGREDIENTS FOR SERVING

1 recipe vanilla bean ice cream (Follow the recipe for Jack Daniels
   vanilla ice cream, page 209, but leave out the whiskey.)

1 recipe pear sauce (page 220)

1 recipe butterscotch sauce (Make bourbon butterscotch sauce, page 218,
   omitting the bourbon.)

PREPARATION FOR THE CAKE

1. Preheat oven to 350°.

2. Thoroughly butter a 10-inch Bundt pan. Dust with flour, shaking out excess.
   Set the pan aside.

3. Sift together the flour, baking powder, and salt. Reserve.

4. Cream the butter with the orange zest and vanilla extract, very gradually adding
   the brown sugar until the mixture is smooth and light.

5. Add the eggs, one at a time, mixing just enough to incorporate after each
   addition.

6. Add the reserved flour mixture, alternating with the milk and pear brandy,
   stopping occasionally to scrape the bowl thoroughly.

7. Stir in the diced pears and place the batter in the prepared pan.

8. Bake for approximately 1 hour and 25 minutes. The cake will be golden brown
   and firm to the touch; it will be just starting to pull away from the sides of the
   pan and will "test done" with a cake tester or skewer, which will come out clean
   when inserted in the cake.

9. Cool the cake in the pan for 10 minutes. Meanwhile, combine the sugar and
   pear brandy in a small saucepan to make the glaze. Cook over low heat until the
   mixture comes to a simmer and the sugar just dissolves.

10. Turn the cake out of the pan. With a pastry brush, brush the warm glaze over
    the entire surface of the cake. Allow to cool.

Note: This cake is actually better made a day in advance. It will keep well for several
days if well wrapped. Different fruits can be substituted for the pears; you might try
apples, cranberries, or blueberries, for example. Nuts can be added in lieu of fruit, and,
as in most recipes, you can vary the spicing and alcohol components if you wish.

Banana Pecan Crostata

This is a great user-friendly recipe. Although somewhat delicate in texture, the pastry for this rustic tart is very easy to work with because you just fold it up around the filling. It requires very little handling, and using a "giant spatula" (see The Art of Pie, below) makes the process a snap. At the Grill, we serve this with a scoop of Jack Daniels vanilla ice cream and a drizzle of bourbon butterscotch sauce.

INGREDIENTS FOR THE CROSTATA DOUGH

1¾ cups flour

2 tablespoons sugar

1 teaspoon cinnamon

¼ teaspoon salt

½ cup lightly toasted pecan pieces

3 ounces unsalted butter, chilled, in pieces

2 ounces vegetable shortening, chilled, in pieces

1 egg

2 tablespoons heavy cream

INGREDIENTS FOR THE TART FILLING

2 tablespoons finely chopped, lightly toasted pecan pieces

½ teaspoon cinnamon

¼ cup sugar

4–5 ripe but firm bananas

1 tablespoon unsalted butter, chilled, in small pieces

fresh nutmeg

INGREDIENTS FOR SERVING

1 recipe Jack Daniels vanilla ice cream (page 209)

1 recipe bourbon butterscotch sauce (page 218)

powdered sugar

PREPARATION FOR THE CROSTATA DOUGH

1. Place the flour, sugar, cinnamon, salt, and pecans in a food processor with a steel blade. Pulse to combine until the nuts are finely ground.
2. Add the butter and shortening to the processor bowl and pulse until they are cut in and the mixture resembles coarse meal.
3. Add the egg and cream to the processor bowl and pulse until the dough just comes together. Do not overwork!
4. Remove the dough, gather it into a round, and flatten. Wrap in plastic and chill several hours or overnight.

ASSEMBLY

1. Preheat oven to 400°. Remove the dough from the refrigerator and let sit at room temperature for 10 minutes.
2. On a lightly floured surface, roll the dough out into a circle approximately

⅛ inch thick and 12 inches in diameter. Place the dough on a parchment paper–lined cookie or baking sheet. Sprinkle the finely chopped pecan pieces over the dough surface, leaving an outer border of 1½ inches.

3. Combine the cinnamon and sugar and sprinkle approximately ⅔ of this mixture over the entire dough surface.

4. Slice the bananas into pieces approximately ¼ inch thick. Preserving the 1½-inch outer border, place the bananas in an overlapping pattern on the pastry dough.

5. Sprinkle the bananas with the remaining cinnamon and sugar, dot with the butter pieces, and grate a bit of fresh nutmeg over the top of the tart.

6. Fold the border of the dough up over the bananas, forming the sides of the tart, folding and pleating as you go. Press on the dough, gently, to secure the sides.

7. Bake approximately 25 minutes, until the dough is golden brown.

8. Dust the tart with powdered sugar and serve warm with ice cream and butterscotch sauce.

The Art of Pie

OK, I confess that I have been on a long-term mission to convince people to bake more at home. I'm not talking complicated tortes and pastries; I mean something along the lines of your basic pie. A simple fruit pie is often a daunting challenge even to experienced cooks because of a widespread fear of pastry. The key to great pie is in the crust.

The making of pie crust is often an intuitive skill for innate bakers. Still, my family did not make pies, with the exception of my mother's chocolate pudding pie in a graham cracker crumb crust, and yet somehow I taught myself to make them. I've always attributed my pie making success to the fact that I have "very cold hands" and a relaxed attitude toward baking. I have been told that I "have the gift"—you see, in the South, having a good touch with pastry is a much-admired talent in certain circles. When faced with attending my first big family reunion (on Ben's side), I hid my nervousness behind my pies (double-crusted blueberry blackberry). I grew up a world away from northern Alamance County, and yet I was immediately accepted into this tightly knit clan. I can't help but feel that the pies had something to do with it.

Pie making is a process that is often better observed than described. It is a skill that used to be handed down within a family, and unfortunately it is becoming something of a lost art. While there is no accompanying instructional video, the following detailed tips should put you on the proper path to humble, delicious pie.

- The number one secret to good pie crust is *cold*. Chill all ingredients before using. I precut my butter and shortening and freeze them for 15 to 20 minutes before using. Note that I use a combination of butter and shortening for a balance of flavor (from the butter) and flakiness (from the shortening).
- Use a food processor, if you have one, to cut the fat into your dry ingredient mixture. I have found that using the steel blade in short quick pulses is absolutely the most effective way to accomplish this task.
- If you've used a processor to cut in the fat, transfer the fat-flour mixture to a large mixing bowl to add the water manually. People tend to overwork the dough when using the processor for this step. You have much more control doing it by hand.
- Place ice water in a squeeze bottle with a narrow tip (the kind that mustard or ketchup often comes in). Again, this will give you better control, and you will be less likely to overwet the dough.
- Gradually "stir" water into the flour mixture, using a fork in a quick "scrambling motion." Continue to add water and toss the flour mixture, turning your bowl until the dough is evenly moistened and cleanly comes together when lightly squeezed. It should have the consistency of play-dough—moist, not crumbly but not wet or sticky.
- Shape the dough into a flattened disc before wrapping and chilling. It is much easier to roll the dough into a round shape if you start with a round shape. Chill the

dough thoroughly before rolling and remove it from the refrigerator 5 minutes before using.

· I like to "roll" my pie dough by actually pounding it to flatten, giving the dough quarter turns to ensure even thickness. Lift and lightly flour under the dough frequently. Once the dough is fairly thin, complete by actually rolling, working from the center to the edge.

· To maneuver my dough as I work with it, I use a wonderful tool distributed by the King Arthur Flour Company (see Sources) called a giant spatula. A thin rimless cookie sheet or metal pizza peel works equally well. You can slide the spatula right under the dough to move or turn it, preventing sticking and cracking. It is particularly useful for transferring rolled dough into a pie pan or picking up a top crust and placing it over a prepared filling.

· Always place juicy fruit pies on foil or a cookie sheet before baking to avoid a messy oven in the event of spillovers.

· While crust is critical to a successful pie, the filling component is equally important. Always use ripe (but not soft), fragrant seasonal fruit.

· When making single-crusted pies, partially bake the crust prior to filling to attain a crisp bottom. This process, commonly known as "baking blind," is particularly important when making cream or custard-based pies. To do this, roll out the crust and line the pie pan. Chill or freeze until the dough is firm. Place a generous sheet of parchment paper (aluminum foil will work but parchment is preferable) over the crust and weight it down with pie weights, rice, or dried beans. The edges of the parchment should come up over the rim of the pie plate to facilitate removal. Place the weighted crust in a preheated 350° to 375° oven and bake approximately 15 minutes. Once the pastry is set and loses its raw look, carefully remove the parchment and weights. Place the pie shell back in the oven. Check after 2 minutes to see if the pastry has developed any air bubbles. If it has, gently prick them with a fork. Repeat the process after another minute or two. Bake until the crust is lightly golden.

Blueberry-Peach (or Nectarine) Pie

MAKES 1 9-INCH PIE; SERVES 8

A good pie is one of our favorite desserts—and it makes for a rather wonderful breakfast item too! There are few things better than a warm slice of freshly baked pie, unless it's that piece of pie topped with a generous scoop of homemade ice cream. In this case, we suggest peach ice cream (page 210). At Magnolia Grill we are known for our homey repertoire of pies, crisps, buckles, crumbles, cobblers, and betties, which always showcase whatever fruit is in peak season. We hand choose our fruit, making sure that it's fragrant and ripe. Follow the wise advice of Karen's grandmother: the best fruit is not always the prettiest. This combination of peaches and blueberries produces a pie with fabulous flavor and texture. Feel free to substitute nectarines for the peaches (no need to skin them) or vary the berry type if you wish.

This recipe gives you ample pastry for a generous double-crusted pie. It is easier for the novice baker to have a bit more pastry than necessary to facilitate the rolling process, so be careful to roll the dough to the proper thickness.

INGREDIENTS FOR THE PIE CRUST

    2⅔ cups flour
    ¾ teaspoon salt
    ¾ tablespoon sugar
    4 ounces chilled unsalted butter, cut into pieces
    4 ounces chilled vegetable shortening, cut into pieces
    approximately ¼–½ cup cold water, or as needed

INGREDIENTS FOR THE FILLING

    2 pints fresh blueberries
    1 pound fresh, ripe, but firm peaches, blanched, peeled,
        and sliced ¾ inch thick (approximately 2 cups)
    ¾ cup sugar, or to taste
    6 tablespoons flour
    zest of 1 orange, grated
    juice of 1 orange
    ¼ teaspoon cinnamon
    ¼ teaspoon nutmeg
    ¼ teaspoon ground cloves
    ¼ teaspoon salt

INGREDIENTS FOR THE EGG GLAZE

    1 egg yolk
    1 teaspoon water

PREPARATION FOR THE PIE CRUST

    1. Place the flour, salt, and sugar in the bowl of a food processor with a steel
       blade. Pulse to combine.

2. Add the chilled butter and shortening; pulse until the fat is evenly cut in and the mixture resembles coarse cornmeal. Remove to a mixing bowl.

3. Working quickly, gradually add cold water while tossing and stirring the dough with a fork until it just begins to come together. Divide the dough into two even portions, flatten into rounds, wrap in plastic, and chill for several hours or overnight.

PREPARATION FOR THE PIE

1. Preheat oven to 400°.

2. Combine the egg yolk and water to make a glaze for the top crust. Reserve.

3. Combine all of the filling ingredients and toss gently to mix well.

4. Working quickly, roll out the bottom crust approximately ¼ inch thick and fit into a 9-inch glass pie pan.

5. Place the fruit into the crust, mounding slightly in the center.

6. Roll out the top crust.

7. Trim excess overhang from the bottom crust and brush the remaining edges lightly with water. Cover the filling with the top crust. Fold the edges of the top crust under the pie, pressing well to seal. Scallop the edges of the crust. Brush the crust with the egg wash glaze. Cut steam vents in the top crust.

8. Place the pie on a baking sheet or piece of foil to catch possible juice spills.

9. Bake at 400° for approximately 30 minutes. Reduce the oven setting to 375° and bake for an additional 20 to 30 minutes, until the juices are bubbling and the crust is golden brown.

Deep-Dish Apple Cinnamon Crisp
with Brandied Vanilla Ice Cream

SERVES 6

This falls into the category of what we call "warm somethings with ice cream." Apple crisp is a time-honored classic that seems to satisfy everyone. It is consistently one of the best sellers whenever it makes an appearance on our dessert menu. While there's something to be said for simplicity, you can add some raisins, dates, or sun-dried cherries to the apple filling if you wish.

INGREDIENTS FOR THE CRISP TOPPING

1 cup flour

1 cup sugar

½ teaspoon cinnamon

¼ teaspoon nutmeg

⅛ teaspoon salt

½ cup old-fashioned oats

8 tablespoons cold unsalted butter, cut into pieces

INGREDIENTS FOR THE APPLE FILLING

6 cups Granny Smith apples, peeled, cored,
    and sliced ¼ inch thick (about 6–7 apples)

½ cup sugar

1 tablespoon flour

¾ teaspoon cinnamon

⅛ teaspoon salt

zest of 1 orange, grated

2 teaspoons orange juice

INGREDIENT FOR SERVING

1 recipe brandied vanilla ice cream (Follow the recipe for Jack Daniels
    vanilla ice cream, page 209, but substitute brandy for the bourbon.)

PREPARATION FOR THE CRISP TOPPING

Combine all of the ingredients except the butter in a food processor. Pulse to combine. Add the butter and pulse until the mixture has the texture of rough meal and clumps together when squeezed lightly. Do not overmix! Reserve while preparing the apple filling.

Note: This step can be done by hand by rubbing the butter into the dry ingredients until the desired consistency is reached. The texture will be a bit coarser since the oats will be left in larger pieces if done this way.

PREPARATION FOR THE APPLE FILLING

1. Preheat oven to 350°.
2. Combine all of the filling ingredients and toss lightly to mix.

3. Divide the apples among 6 buttered 1-cup ceramic ramekins (for individual servings) or a buttered deep 9 × 9-inch baking dish.

4. Gently squeeze handfuls of the crisp topping together and place on top of the apple filling, pressing lightly to make the crisp adhere.

5. Place the ramekins or baking dish on a foil-lined baking sheet and bake for approximately 35 minutes, until the juices are bubbling, the crisp topping is lightly brown, and the apples are soft when pierced with a paring knife.

6. Serve warm with brandied vanilla ice cream. This can be made several hours ahead and reheated lightly just before serving.

Maple View Dairy Buttermilk Cheesecake

MAKES 1 10-INCH CAKE; SERVES 10 TO 12

Ben remembers eating cornbread crumbled into a bowl of buttermilk as a childhood snack. Karen remembers New York–style cheesecake being a family favorite. The synthesis of these two memories showcases Maple View Dairy buttermilk—this is the real stuff that comes in old-fashioned glass bottles. While any buttermilk can be used, if you have an artisanal dairy in your area, we recommend using its product. Farm-style buttermilk is thicker, richer, and more complex in flavor. Even if you are not a buttermilk lover, give this recipe a try. It is wonderful served with fresh, seasonal berries; sliced, lightly sugared peaches; or a fresh blueberry compote (page 219).

INGREDIENTS

    1 ½ cups graham cracker crumbs

    ½ cup yellow cornmeal

    2 tablespoons sugar (for crust) + 1 cup sugar (for cheesecake)

    3 ounces unsalted butter, melted

    4 ounces unsalted butter, at room temperature

    1 ½ pounds cream cheese, at room temperature

    zest of 2 lemons, grated

    ¾ cup buttermilk

    1 teaspoon vanilla extract

    4 eggs

PREPARATION

1. Preheat oven to 350°. Butter a 10-inch springform pan.

2. Combine the graham cracker crumbs, cornmeal, 2 tablespoons sugar, and 3 ounces melted butter. Press the mixture into the bottom and 1 inch up the sides of the pan. Bake for approximately 10 minutes, until lightly golden. Reserve.

3. Cream the room-temperature butter and cream cheese with the lemon zest and 1 cup sugar until smooth. Add the buttermilk and vanilla. Beat, scraping the bowl occasionally, until well combined.

4. Add the eggs and slowly beat just to combine. Do not overmix.

5. Pour into the reserved crust. Bake 25 minutes, then turn oven down to 300° and bake an additional 25 minutes. Turn oven to the low setting and bake until done (approximately 20 more minutes—the cake will be set around the edges and barely jiggly in the very center). Cool and chill several hours before serving. Serve with a mixture of seasonal fresh berries.

Chocolate-Raspberry Soufflé Cake

MAKES 1 10½-INCH CAKE, OR 10 TO 12 PORTIONS

Attention chocoholics! This raspberry-flavored chocolate cake is like an intense giant truffle. In reality it is a rich, fudgey, fallen soufflé. It is a wonderful special occasion cake and can be decorated in a myriad of ways. If you prefer, an alternative liquid can be substituted for the raspberry sauce. A mixture of cognac and crème de cacao is particularly delicious.

INGREDIENTS FOR THE CAKE

11 ounces semisweet chocolate, cut into small pieces

14 tablespoons unsalted butter

1 cup sugar, divided

7 eggs, separated

½ cup flour

1 recipe raspberry sauce (page 220), divided (with some reserved for final plating)

⅛ teaspoon salt

INGREDIENTS FOR THE CHOCOLATE GANACHE TOPPING

⅜ cup heavy cream

6 ounces semisweet chocolate, cut into small pieces

INGREDIENTS FOR PRESENTATION

powdered sugar

unsweetened cocoa powder

lightly sweetened whipped cream (page 221)

reserved raspberry sauce

PREPARATION FOR THE CAKE

1. Remove the top rack from the oven. Place the bottom rack at the lowest position. Preheat oven to 350°.
2. Grease a 10½-inch springform pan with vegetable shortening. Line the bottom of the pan with a round piece of parchment paper and grease the paper. Cut 2 strips of parchment 6 inches wide × 12 inches long. Lightly grease both sides of the strips with shortening and use them to line the interior sides of the springform pan, forming a collar as if you were making a soufflé. Vegetable shortening works much better for doing this than butter does! Dust the pan and collar with flour, lightly knocking out excess.
3. Combine the chocolate with the butter in the top of a double boiler and melt over low heat.

4. Meanwhile, combine ¾ cup sugar with the egg yolks and whip until very thick and pale. Carefully add the melted chocolate to the egg yolks and whip to combine. Add the flour slowly. Add ⅜ cup of the raspberry sauce. Transfer this mixture to a large stainless bowl.

5. Whip the egg whites with the salt until foamy. Gradually add ¼ cup sugar and whip until the whites form soft peaks. Fold a third of the egg whites into the chocolate mixture to lighten. Quickly but thoroughly fold in the remaining egg whites. Pour the batter into the prepared pan and place the pan in the oven.

6. Bake for approximately 40 minutes. The cake will rise up and appear soufflé-like. The top will be a bit crusty and may just start to crack. If tested with a skewer, the cake center will appear very moist—almost liquidlike—but it *is* done. Do not overbake! Remove from the oven and allow to cool thoroughly in the pan. The cake will deflate and fall as it cools.

7. Remove the sides of the springform pan and the parchment collar. Invert the cake onto a cardboard cake circle or parchment-lined plate. Remove the springform bottom and parchment paper and reinvert the cake onto a service plate or another cardboard round. Prepare the ganache topping.

PREPARATION FOR THE CHOCOLATE GANACHE TOPPING

1. Heat the cream in a medium saucepan till just under a boil. Add the chocolate and cook over very low heat, stirring, until the chocolate is completely melted.

2. Remove from heat and place over an ice bath, stirring until the mixture reaches a spreadable consistency. Please note that you can make the ganache topping ahead of time. It will keep refrigerated for up to 4 days. Allow it to reach room temperature and spreadable consistency before using.

3. To ice the cake, dollop small spoonfuls of ganache over the top and, using a palate knife or metal spatula, smooth out the ganache, taking it just up to the edge of the cake. For a finished look, lightly create a zigzag pattern on the top of the cake and run a palate knife around the top edge to smooth out the ganache. Place the cake in the refrigerator just long enough to set the ganache (10 to 15 minutes). Remove from the refrigerator and sprinkle lightly with powdered sugar and unsweetened cocoa powder.

4. Serve the cake at room temperature accompanied by whipped cream and the remaining raspberry sauce.

Note: For a more opulent presentation, you can cover the entire surface of the cake with concentric circles of fresh raspberries before you allow the ganache to set. If you choose to do this, forgo the sprinkling of cocoa powder and just garnish with a bit of powdered sugar.

Ginger-Lime Crème Caramels with Tropical Ambrosia

MAKES 6 SERVINGS IN 1-CUP RAMEKINS

In this recipe an old classic is updated with tropical flavors. Ginger and lime provide a refreshing foil to the rich custard. You can bake the crème caramels in individual 1-cup ovenproof ramekins or in a 6-cup ceramic soufflé dish. If choosing the larger format, you will have to adjust the baking time accordingly—it will probably take an additional 20 minutes. Ambrosia is familiar fare on many traditional Southern holiday dessert tables. While many recipe variations can be found, all seem to incorporate oranges and coconut. You can garnish individual plates with the fruit mélange or simply set out a bowl and allow folks to help themselves.

INGREDIENTS FOR THE CARAMEL

> 1½ cups sugar
> ⅝ cup water, divided
> ¼ cup lime juice

INGREDIENTS FOR THE CUSTARD

> 3 cups half-and-half
> 4 eggs
> 4 egg yolks
> ¾ cup sugar
> 2 tablespoons + 1 teaspoon ginger purée (page 248)
> zest of 2 limes, grated
> 1 teaspoon ground ginger
> ¼ teaspoon salt
> 1 teaspoon vanilla extract
> 1 tablespoon lime juice

INGREDIENTS FOR THE AMBROSIA

> 2 navel oranges, all peel and pith removed, cut into segments
> 1 cup fresh pineapple, cut into ½-inch dice
> 1 mango, peeled and cut into ½-inch dice
> 1 kiwi fruit, peeled, quartered, and sliced ¼ inch thick
> ½ cup sweetened coconut shreds, lightly toasted

PREPARATION FOR THE CARAMEL

> 1. Have 6 ceramic ramekins (or a soufflé dish) easily accessible. Combine the sugar and ½ cup of the water in a heavy saucepot. Bring to a boil without stirring: you can swirl the pan to distribute the syrup as it starts picking up color.
> 2. Meanwhile, combine the lime juice and the other ⅛ cup of water in a small saucepan and bring to just under a boil.

3. When the caramel syrup is evenly amber in color, add the hot lime juice–water mixture to the caramel; the caramel may steam and spatter, so be careful. Swirl the pan and immediately divide the caramel syrup between the ramekins (or place it in a 6-cup soufflé dish). Tilt each ramekin so that the syrup coats the bottom and sides. Allow to cool for 10 minutes. Meanwhile, make the custard.

PREPARATION FOR THE CUSTARD

1. Preheat oven to 325°. Place the half-and-half in a saucepan and bring to just under a boil. Reserve.

2. In a stainless steel mixing bowl, whisk together the eggs, egg yolks, sugar, ginger purée, lime zest, ground ginger, salt, vanilla, and lime juice.

3. Add a bit of the hot half-and-half to the egg mixture and whisk to temper the eggs. Whisk in the remaining half-and-half. Strain the mixture through a fine sieve. Divide the custard evenly between the ramekins.

4. Place the ramekins in a large baking pan. Place the baking pan on a rack in the middle of the oven. Fill the pan with water so that it comes halfway up the sides of the ramekins. Cover the pan with aluminum foil. Bake until the custards are just set around the edges but still a bit jiggly in the center. This should take approximately 50 minutes, but start checking for doneness after 40 minutes and check every 5 minutes thereafter. Baking times on custards can vary from batch to batch. Remove the ramekins from the baking pan when the custards are done. Refrigerate a minimum of 4 hours or overnight.

5. Unmold the custards before serving. Run a thin-bladed paring knife around the inside edge of each ramekin to loosen the custard. Invert the custard onto a plate. Serve with tropical ambrosia.

PREPARATION FOR THE AMBROSIA

Place all the ingredients in a bowl and mix lightly to combine.

Note: Working with caramel is not difficult, but it does necessitate being careful. For proper flavor you want to take caramel to the point of being evenly amber in color. If you undercook it, it will taste washed out; if you overcook it, it will taste burnt. To remove stubborn, sticky, hardened caramel from the ramekins once you have turned the custards out, fill the ramekins with water and place them in a 300° to 350° oven until the sugar softens and dissolves.

Double Chocolate Waffles with Strawberries & White Chocolate Ice Cream

SERVES 10 TO 12

This dessert is something of a cross between strawberry shortcake and an ice cream sandwich. Modeled after waffles à la mode, an old Brooklyn diner favorite, it's a great dessert to make if you have access to local strawberries. While more perishable than commercial varieties, native berries tend to be juicier, sweeter, and more fragrant.

INGREDIENTS FOR THE WAFFLES

    1 cup flour

    ¼ cup unsweetened cocoa powder

    1 ¼ teaspoons baking powder

    ¼ teaspoon baking soda

    ⅛ teaspoon salt

    ½ cup sugar

    3 ½ tablespoons unsalted butter

    2 ½ ounces semisweet chocolate, chopped

    2 eggs

    1 cup + 2 tablespoons milk

    ½ teaspoon vanilla extract

    1 ½ tablespoons crème de cacao (or other liqueur)

INGREDIENTS FOR PRESENTATION

    2 ½ pints strawberries

    sugar to taste

    1 recipe white chocolate ice cream (page 211)

    1 recipe bittersweet chocolate sauce (see page 217)

    powdered sugar

PREPARATION FOR THE WAFFLES

1. Sift the flour, cocoa powder, baking powder, baking soda, salt, and sugar into a large bowl.

2. Combine the butter and semisweet chocolate in a double boiler. Place over low heat until melted. Whisk in the eggs; whisk in the milk, vanilla, and crème de cacao.

3. Make a well in the center of the dry ingredients and gradually whisk in the milk mixture.

4. Using a waffle iron and following the manufacturer's instructions, make waffles with the chocolate batter. The waffles will be somewhat soft when first removed from the waffle iron—they will crisp as they cool. The waffles can be made ahead. Store, wrapped and refrigerated, for up to 2 days. Bring back to room temperature before using.

PRESENTATION

1. Preheat oven to 350°.

2. Hull the strawberries, cut them into thick slices, and sugar them to taste. Reserve.

3. Cut the waffles into triangles, place on a baking sheet, and toast lightly (about 5 minutes).

4. Sprinkle dessert plates with powdered sugar and drizzle with chocolate sauce. For each serving, place 1 waffle triangle on a plate and top with a spoonful of strawberries and a scoop of ice cream; top this with another waffle triangle, more berries, and a second scoop of ice cream. Drizzle the top scoop of ice cream with some additional chocolate sauce and place a few sliced berries on each plate.

Jack Daniels Vanilla Ice Cream

The dessert department at the Grill has been known to add seriously to overall liquor costs by virtue of using alcohol as a flavoring agent. While this ice cream sans whiskey is good, the addition of a generous quantity of fine Tennessee sour mash makes it downright delicious.

INGREDIENTS
- 3 ¾ cups half-and-half
- 3 cups heavy cream
- 1 ½ large vanilla beans
- 14 egg yolks
- 1 ½ cups sugar
- ¼ teaspoon salt
- ½ cup Jack Daniels whiskey or good quality bourbon

PREPARATION
1. Place the half-and-half and cream in a large stainless steel saucepan. Split the vanilla beans and scrape the seeds into the cream mixture. Add the vanilla bean pods to the cream as well. Bring the cream to just under a boil over medium heat.
2. Combine the egg yolks, sugar, and salt in a stainless bowl and whisk to combine. Temper the egg yolk mixture by stirring in some of the hot cream. Transfer the egg yolk mixture to the saucepan and cook, stirring, over low heat until the mixture thickens slightly (nappé stage). Remove from heat.
3. Strain the ice cream base into another container and cool down over an ice bath. Stir in the whiskey and freeze in an ice cream machine following the manufacturer's directions.

Peach Ice Cream

Peach ice cream always conjures up visions of hot summer days, shady porches, and old wooden White Mountain–style hand crank ice cream machines. While we don't churn our ice cream the old-fashioned way, savoring a scoop of this "frozen custard" can transport you back to simpler times.

INGREDIENTS

2⅓ pounds ripe, fragrant peaches, blanched, peeled, and sliced

2 tablespoons + 2 teaspoons lemon juice

1 500-milligram vitamin C tablet (see hint)

1⅔ cups sugar, divided

⅓ cup peach schnapps or brandy

2⅔ cups half-and-half

2⅔ cups heavy cream

11 egg yolks

¼ teaspoon salt

1 tablespoon + 1 teaspoon vanilla extract

PREPARATION

1. In a stainless saucepot, combine the sliced peaches, lemon juice, and vitamin C tablet. Cook, stirring, over medium heat until the peaches are soft and heated through. Remove from heat and stir in ⅔ cup sugar and the peach schnapps. Mash the peaches until they break up into small pieces. Allow the mixture to macerate at room temperature for 1 hour.

2. Place the half-and-half and cream in a large stainless saucepot and bring to just under a boil over medium heat.

3. Meanwhile, combine the egg yolks, 1 cup sugar, and the salt in a mixing bowl and whisk to combine. Temper the egg yolk mixture with some of the hot cream. Combine egg yolks with the cream in the saucepot and cook, stirring over gentle heat until the mixture thickens (nappé stage). Remove from heat.

4. Strain the mixture into another container and cool down over an ice bath. Add the vanilla and the reserved peach mixture. Freeze in an ice cream machine following the manufacturer's directions.

Hint: By cooking the peaches with a vitamin C tablet, you avoid discoloration from oxidation without adding the flavor of a large quantity of an acidic liquid such as lemon juice. This trick works for all fruits that have a tendency to turn brown, such as apricots, apples, and pears, among others. It is especially useful to remember when poaching fruit, preparing sauces, or making purées in which you want to maintain a particular color profile.

White Chocolate Ice Cream

MAKES A HALF GALLON

We're not huge fans of white chocolate, but this recipe does produce a beautiful rich, creamy ice cream that is extremely versatile. It is wonderful when topped with a simple raspberry sauce or used instead of whipped cream in any traditional strawberry shortcake recipe. Pairing it with peaches or cherries also works well. A chocolate chip variation is another option, giving the ice cream a totally different flavor/texture profile.

INGREDIENTS

    3 ½ cups half-and-half

    3 ½ cups heavy cream

    18 ounces white chocolate, finely chopped

    12 egg yolks

    ½ cup sugar

    ¼ teaspoon salt

    ⅓ cup light or dark crème de cacao

    1 ½ cups semisweet chocolate, cut into small chunks (optional)

PREPARATION

1. Place the half-and-half and cream in a large stainless steel saucepan and bring to just under a boil over medium heat.

2. Remove the cream mixture from the heat and add the white chocolate. Stir until the chocolate melts. Reserve.

3. Place the egg yolks, sugar, and salt in a mixing bowl and whisk to combine. Temper the egg yolk mixture by stirring in some of the hot cream. Combine the egg yolks with the cream in the saucepan and cook, stirring, over low heat, until the mixture thickens slightly (nappé stage). Remove from heat.

4. Strain the ice cream base into another container and cool down over an ice bath. Stir in the crème de cacao and freeze in an ice cream machine following the manufacturer's directions.

5. If you choose to include the optional chocolate chips, you can add them to the partially frozen ice cream base during the freezing process or fold them into the finished, frozen ice cream before storing, depending on your individual machine's instructions. For the most fabulous chips, make your own using premium quality semisweet chocolate. Melt the chocolate and then pour it out onto a parchment-lined baking sheet. Allow the chocolate to just barely set. Score it into ¼-inch chips with a knife and refrigerate, on the parchment, till completely set. Turn upside down and remove the parchment. Break apart the individual chips and store them in an airtight container.

Watermelon Granita

MAKES APPROXIMATELY 2 QUARTS

Remember those summer potlucks where someone brought a spiked watermelon for dessert/cocktail hour? In this slightly more sophisticated version you really don't taste the vodka at all—it's added to maintain proper granular consistency when the granita is frozen.

INGREDIENTS

4½ cups watermelon purée—made by seeding, puréeing,
   and straining the flesh of approximately ½ of a small watermelon
   by passing it through a food mill or fine sieve
¾ cup sugar (or to taste)
⅛ teaspoon salt
1½ tablespoons lime juice (or to taste)
⅛ cup vodka
1 recipe brown edge wafer cookies (page 217; optional)

PREPARATION

1. Combine the sugar with 1 cup of the watermelon purée in a saucepan and heat to dissolve the sugar. Please note that the given amount of sugar is a guideline—you might need slightly more or slightly less depending on the sweetness of the watermelon. You can always add a bit less to begin with and then adjust the sugar to taste if you want more.

2. Combine the sugar-watermelon mixture with the remaining watermelon purée and the salt, lime juice, and vodka. Taste the mixture and add additional lime juice or sugar if necessary. The frozen granita will taste slightly less sweet than the unfrozen mix.

3. Pour the mixture into a chilled metal pan and freeze for approximately 45 minutes or until ice crystals begin to form around the edges. Stir the ice crystals into the center of the pan and place back in the freezer. Continue to freeze, stirring every 30 minutes, until the mixture is completely frozen. It will have an icy, slushy, granular texture. Place in a covered container until ready to serve. Stir lightly before serving.

Note: Watermelon granita is a wonderfully refreshing summer treat. At Magnolia Grill we serve it along with a cantaloupe sherbet and brown edge wafer cookies. Topping a mixture of watermelon, honeydew, and cantaloupe balls with the granita is another presentation idea.

Concord Grape Sorbet

MAKES A HALF GALLON

We like to serve several scoops of this sorbet in frosted chilled dessert coupes garnished with white grape jello (see recipe directly below) and Thompson seedless grapes. Pairing the sorbet with old-fashioned peanut butter cookies (page 216) updates the beloved flavor combination of PB&J.

INGREDIENTS

    3 pounds (8 cups) Concord grapes
    ¼ teaspoon salt
    ¼ teaspoon ground cloves
    1 cup dark grape juice (Welch's is fine)
    ¼ cup crème de cassis
    3 tablespoons lime juice
    2 tablespoons orange juice
    1 cup sugar syrup (see note)

PREPARATION

1. Combine the grapes, salt, cloves, and grape juice in a large saucepot. Cook over medium heat, stirring occasionally, until the grapes pop, exude their juices, and are very soft. Remove from heat; pass the mixture through a food mill or purée and strain through a fine-mesh sieve. Discard the grape skins.
2. Cool the grape mixture. Add the cassis, lime juice, orange juice, and sugar syrup. Taste and adjust the seasoning.
3. Freeze the sorbet mix in an ice cream machine according to the manufacturer's directions. Store the frozen sorbet in the freezer for several hours, or for up to several days, before serving.

Note: We always keep a basic 1:1 sugar syrup around for seasoning sorbet mixes. It's also great for sweetening lemonade or iced tea or for moistening sponge cakes. You can make it by combining 3 cups of sugar and 3 cups of water in a saucepot and bringing them to a boil, stirring occasionally. Cook over medium heat until the sugar dissolves. Cool and store in the refrigerator. It keeps forever.

White Grape Jello

FILLS AN 8 × 8-INCH PAN

Say the word "Jello" and people tend to laugh. Given that Karen's first childhood cookbook was a collection of Jello gelatin and pudding recipes, it seems fitting to include this version of the timeless treat. Homemade gelatins based on fresh fruit purées and good quality store-bought juices make wonderful light desserts and sophisticated jewel-like garnishes. Less sweet, not quite as neon-colored, and additive-free, these updated jigglers will please adults as well as kids.